D1067958

Lineberger Memorial

Library

Given By

the estate of the
Rev. Dr. J. Benjamin Bedenbaugh

Lutheran Theological Southern Seminary   Columbia, S. C.

943 212

THE
FIVE BOOKS
OF
MOSES
FOR
YOUNG PEOPLE

943 212

THE
FIVE BOOKS
OF
MOSES
FOR
YOUNG PEOPLE

written and illustrated by
Esta Cassway

JASON ARONSON INC.
Northvale, New Jersey
London

This book was set in 14 point Bem by Lind Graphics of Upper Saddle River, New Jersey, and printed by Haddon Craftsmen of Scranton, Pennsylvania.

Copyright © 1992 by Esta Cassway

10   9   8   7   6   5   4   3   2   1

All rights reserved. Printed in the United States of America. No part of this book may be used or reproduced in any manner whatsoever without written permission from Jason Aronson Inc. except in the case of brief quotations in reviews for inclusion in a magazine, newspaper, or broadcast.

Library of Congress Cataloging-in-Publication Data

Cassway, Esta.
   The five books of Moses for young people / by Esta
Cassway.
     p. cm.
   Summary: Retells the stories found in the first five books of the
Old Testament.
   ISBN 0-87668-451-7
   1. Bible stories, English—O.T. Pentateuch. [1. Bible stories-
-O.T. Pentateuch.] I. Title.
BS551.2.C38 1992
222′.109505—dc20
                                       92-8013
                                         CIP
                                         AC

Manufactured in the United States of America. Jason Aronson Inc. offers books and cassettes. For information and catalog write to Jason Aronson Inc., 230 Livingston Street, Northvale, New Jersey 07647.

This book is dedicated
to my three sons,
Rustin, Nicholas, and Jordan Cassway,
to their future wives and children,
and to their children's children

Contents

Genesis

Exodus

Leviticus

Numbers

Deuteronomy

Genesis

בראשית

The Creation

Once upon a time there was no time. There was no long ago and there was no before. There was only a great nothing, a big nowhere. It was dark and very quiet. There was no movement except for the soft footsteps of God, the Creator, who walked back and forth across this gigantic empty space, thinking.

Many times before, He had tried to make a new world, a place with trees and seas, animals and people, a place where His glorious gifts could grow and live together peacefully. And many times He was not happy with what He had made. Sometimes the colors were not right; the sea was yellow, the sky was green, and the grass came out purple. Sometimes His creatures didn't sound quite right; the cows meowed, the cats mooed, the birds roared, and the lions whistled. Sometimes His creatures behaved in strange ways; the bears walked upside down on their front paws, the fish floated on top of the waves, and the elephants flapped big orange wings and squirted water out of their pink tails.

God said, "This time, I am going to try even harder, and I am going to do this right!"

And this is the story of what He did.

In the beginning, God created the heaven and the earth. Now the earth was bare except for lots and lots of water. God hovered over the waters and said, "Let there be light." And God saw that the light was good. Then God divided the light from the darkness. He called the light "day," a time for work and play, and He called the darkness "night," a time to sleep and dream about daytime. When God saw what He had done, He was very pleased, and made the earth spin around and around so that day and night would return forever. And there was evening and there was morning, a first day.

And God said, "Let there be a sky in the midst of the waters, and let it divide the waters from the waters." God called the sky "heaven" and colored it blue. He collected some of the waters together and made fluffy, white clouds. What a beautiful sight it was. And there was evening and there was morning, a second day.

And God said, "Let the waters under the heaven be gathered together into one place, and let the dry land appear." And it was so. God called the dry land "earth" and made mountains for skiing, forests for camping, and seashores for building sand castles. He called the gathering together of the waters "seas," with oceans for swimming, lakes for sailing, and ponds for fishing. He even made swamps to hold dangerous creatures such as alligators, which were on his list for another day. And God looked around and saw that so far, it looked good.

Then He said, "Let the earth bring forth grass, and seeds, and fruit-bearing trees." God planned to water the new plants with rain just as soon as He had time to create the rain. Then the earth would be covered with soft, green grass, the sunflowers would awaken, and the seeds would sprout into enough tomatoes, cucumbers, and zucchini to feed a world full of people, that is, if there were any people. God hadn't gotten that far yet. But He was getting things ready.

He invented snacks: the grapes were to dry in the sun and become raisins; when the wheat grew tall it would be made into flour for cookies; and He made sure that there would always be peanuts around, some for the monkeys he was going to create, and some, of course, for peanut butter. And God saw that it was good. And there was evening and there was morning, a third day.

And God said, "Let there be lights in the heaven to divide the day from the night; and let them be for signs and for seasons, and for days and years." And God made the two great lights, the sun and the moon. Now the golden sun was the brightest because it had to shine during worktime and playtime; it is important to see clearly and avoid accidents. Since nighttime was bedtime, the silver moon, with its happy face and gentle glow, made a perfect nightlight that would someday keep watch over whoever might be just a little afraid of the dark.

Then God made the stars, which danced liked millions of candles in the night and helped the moon give light upon the earth.

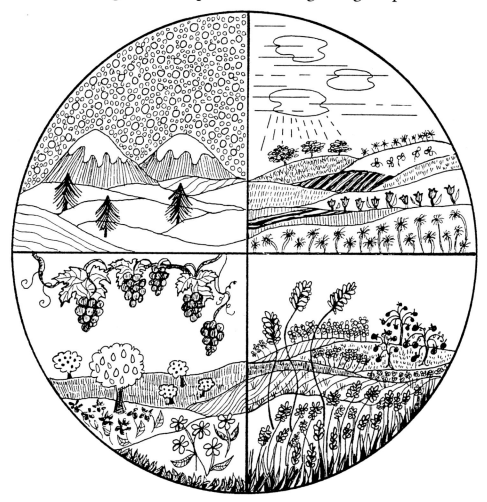

At this time, God also made a calendar. He made years and months, according to where the sun, moon, and stars happened to be. He made seasons for planting and harvesting, for snowballs and snorkeling, for school days and for vacations. This was a very fine idea; since everything was always changing, there would be no time to be bored. And God saw that it was good. And there was evening and there was morning, a fourth day.

And God said, "Let the waters swarm with swarms of living creatures, and let birds fly above the earth in the blue sky." And God created the great whales. They were so big that pelicans and walruses took sightseeing trips on their backs. The whales' spouts were like big water fountains; whitefish and redfish blew bubbles in the foam. While they rode up and down, in and out of the water, the whales sang mysterious songs. Far away, other whales answered them, and beautiful music filled the air. Flounders and tuna fish clapped their fins, and the dolphins did backflips as they followed behind. Swordfish swam along with the parade, their sharp noses in a straight line, one after the other. The great white sharks were the last in line and kept their big mouths shut!

Overhead, the wild geese directed traffic with their honking. Everyone had such a great time on that day; that's why the seagulls are still laughing! God saw that it was good and He was pleased. God blessed them all and said, "Be fruitful and multiply, fill the waters in the seas, and fill the air with birds." And there was evening and there was morning, a fifth day.

And God said, "Let the earth bring forth every kind of living creature: cattle, creeping things, and wild beasts." And it was so.

Big ones and little ones,
Fat ones and skinny,
Tigers and bullfrogs,
And horses that whinney.
Gerbils and turtles,
Skunks and raccoons,
Kangaroos, turkeys,
Bears and baboons.

When God saw that this was good, and that all the animals seemed friendly, He had a wonderful idea: "I shall make all of mankind in My image. They shall take care of the fish of the sea, the birds of the air, and every living thing that creeps upon the earth."

And so God created male and female. He said, "Be fruitful and multiply, and replenish the earth with babies and children who will grow up to enjoy the earth's treasures. I am asking you to take care of all the creatures that I have made. They will be good friends and dear companions. I have given you seeds and fruit trees, and there will be food for all who breathe the breath of life."

From far away, God heard the sound of singing. It was the baby trees singing for joy before God. In the jungles, the lions roared their thanks for giving them such a fine home. In the dry, sandy deserts, the coyotes gave grateful howls for the water holes hidden in the sand. The birds sang sweet lullabies as they sat in their nests, the crickets chanted to the moon, the roosters crowed at the sun, and the turtledove sang love songs to God. The music echoed between the mountains and floated over the seas. God saw that everything He had made was working together and He was delighted. It was very good. And there was evening and there was morning, the sixth day.

Now the heaven and the earth and all those who lived there had been created. On the seventh day, God was finished with all His work. It had been such a big job! He said, "I shall bless the seventh day and make it holy, for on that day I rested from creating the world." God called this special day "The Sabbath," the day of rest and holiness.

Every day is a reminder of God's wonderful creation: the sun rises and sets, night returns, and the moon moves through the heavens. The animals help man gather food that comes from seeds and trees, and man is kind and takes good care of his helpers. Children eat the food and grow up strong and healthy. And they use their lovely voices to say thank you to God for all these glorious gifts.

Adam and Eve

It is good to take a nice, long rest. It helps you feel happy and ready to get back to work. That's how God felt, after His nice, long rest on the seventh day of Creation.

God, the Creator, said, "Now that I've made animals and birds and man in My own image, I'd better water My new plants so that they will grow and become food for everyone."

He caused a wet, foggy mist to come up from the earth and it watered the whole face of the ground. Little seedlings peeked out of the soil and lifted their happy faces to the sun. Tiny trees became bigger trees, and bigger trees became giant trees. Wheat waved hello, beans jumped up and down, and walnuts rolled around bumping into almonds and pecans. The land was very busy.

Next, God took dust from all over His new world and molded it like clay to give man a shape. There was white dust and brown dust, red dust and yellow dust. After He made the body, with fingers and toes and eyebrows and a bellybutton, God did the most amazing thing: He breathed His own breath into man's nostrils and man became a living soul!

God called the man "Adam," which means "From the Earth."

9

Since Adam needed a place to live, God gave him a garden. God picked a good spot facing east, and called it Eden. Then He planted trees. They were all pleasant to see; some of them even grew food that was good to eat. In the middle of the garden He put a very special tree. This was the Tree of Life. It was so tall that it went through the clouds, brushed its branches against the stars, and touched heaven. Around the Tree of Life, He planted another special tree: the Tree of the Knowledge of Good and Evil. It protected the Tree of Life from anyone who thought they could know all things and be like God. Since there is only one God, and He is the One Who gives life, this was a very holy tree.

Next, God created a river to flow through the garden and help keep it green. Everything was lovely; the Garden of Eden, Adam's new home, was ready.

God led Adam into the garden and gave him a job. The first job ever. Adam was to be the gardener. After he was finished working, he could eat some of what he grew. But first God created a rule. He said, "A certain part of this garden is off limits to you. You shall not eat from the Tree of the Knowledge of Good and Evil; for if you do, you shall surely die." This was a very serious rule. God hoped that Adam would listen carefully and obey Him.

God did not want Adam to be alone and so He brought all the animals and birds that He had created to the beautiful Garden of Eden. He gave Adam a second job: he was the Official Name-Giver. The animals lined up and Adam gave each of them name tags made from lily pads. He said, "Hello, your name is Squirrel. Hello, your name is Antelope. Hello, your name is Hippopotamus. Hello, your name is Dog." Some rabbits he named "Bunny," some bears he named "Teddy," and a certain spider was named "Daddy Long Legs." It took a long time but he kept naming. "Hello, your name is Wallaby. Hello, your name is Platypus. Hello, your name is Orangutan. Hello, your name is Rat."

When all the creatures had their name tags, Adam gave a big garden party so that everyone could get to know each other. Adam organized games and they played Leap Frog, Duck Duck Goose, and Pin the Tail on the Donkey, using those sticky seed pods that

fall from trees. They had pony rides and a flea circus, and watched the dancing bears give their very first show. And the food was so good!

There were figs and cherries,
All kinds of berries,
Lemonade, grapejuice,
And olives to munch.
There were carrot sticks,
Oranges, raisins, bananas,
And a big healthy salad
For this big hungry bunch.

But when the party was over, and all the animals and birds and bugs had gone to sleep, Adam looked around and felt lonely; there was no one to talk to in his own language. And even more important than that, there was nobody to hug. God saw all the work Adam had done and was pleased. But He noticed that Adam was sad. He said, "It is not good for man to be alone. He needs a good friend and helper of his own kind, another person."

God caused a deep sleep to fall upon Adam, such a deep sleep that Adam was sure not to wake up for a long time. While Adam slept, God took one of his ribs. And from that rib, God created a female. When Adam woke up he said, "Goodness! Look at this! This is bone of my bone and flesh of my flesh!" Adam named this new being "Woman" because she was taken from man. "She will be my wife," he said.

Adam and his wife were married under the great canopy of the Tree of Life. Everyone was invited: the animals brushed their hair and fur, the birds shined their feathers, the bugs were on their best behavior, and the angels sang heavenly songs.

Now in those days, the serpent was the most clever of all the creatures the Lord God had made.

12

He stood on two feet and was as tall as a camel. He was king over all animals, cattle, and the beasts of the field. But not only was he slippery, he was sly. He had some mean tricks under his skin. The serpent asked Adam's wife, "Has God told you not to eat from any special tree in the garden?"

The woman replied, "We may eat fruit from all the trees except for the fruit of the tree that is in the middle of the garden. God said, 'You shall not eat from this special tree, nor shall you touch it, or you will die.'"

And the serpent said to the woman, "You surely would not die; for God knows that on the day you eat from it your eyes shall be opened, and you shall be like God, knowing good and evil."

Then the serpent pushed the woman against the Tree of the Knowledge of Good and Evil and said, "Look, you touched the tree and nothing happened, so don't be afraid. Nothing is going to happen if you take a bite of this delicious fruit."

He was a sneaky old snake. You see, the woman was slightly confused; she had not paid close attention and had gotten the rule mixed up. God did not say, "Do not touch." He said, "Do not eat." When the woman saw the beautiful tree she was delighted and took a big juicy bite of the fruit, thinking it would make her wise. She gave some to Adam, who, because he was hungry, forgot the rule and ate. Suddenly, both their eyes were opened. Before, they had trusted in God and all was good. Now they understood that there were good things and bad, beautiful and ugly. For the first time, Adam and his wife noticed that they were naked, and they covered themselves with fig leaves: they had learned to be embarrassed.

When they heard God walking in the garden, they knew they were in trouble and hid themselves among the trees. Adam and his wife were very upset. God called to Adam and said, "Where are you?"

Adam answered, "I heard Your voice in the garden and I was afraid because I was naked and I hid."

God said, "Who told you that you were naked? Have you eaten from the tree of which I commanded you not to eat?"

And the man said, "The woman gave me some fruit from the tree, and I ate it." Adam blamed his sin on his wife.

God said to the woman, "What is this you have done?"

And she said, "The serpent tricked me and I ate the fruit." The woman blamed the serpent.

Then God said to the serpent, "Because you have done this, you shall be cursed among the beasts of the field! You shall no longer stand upright but forevermore slither upon your belly and eat dust! You shall no longer have a voice and I shall cut your tongue in two! You shall always lose your scaly skin, and man will fear you and try to kill you! Since you crawl on the ground, people will step on your head!''

God waited a bit to punish Adam and his wife—when people are ashamed about doing a bad deed, it's good to leave them alone for a while to think about what they have done. When God saw that Adam and his wife were calm enough to receive their punishment, this is what He said:

To the woman: "You will now know the feeling called pain; sometimes your body will hurt.''

To Adam: "While you lived in My garden, everything was given to you. It was a paradise. Because you did not follow My rule, you will now have to work hard in fields full of thorns and thistles. You shall not live forever, and at the end of your days, you shall return to the dust from which you came.''

Adam then gave his wife the name Eve, which means "Life''; she would be the mother of all living people. And God took pity on Adam and Eve because all they had to wear were fig leaves. He made pants, a shirt, and a dress from the serpent's skin and clothed them.

God said, "Now man and woman know good from bad. But I cannot depend on them. I do not want them to eat food from the Tree of Life and live forever. So I shall send them away today from this Garden of Eden. If they have learned their lesson well, they will teach their children to follow the rules, especially the rules of God."

When God sent Adam and Eve from the garden, the sun and the stars cried big tears. The animals wept and there was much bleating, barking, and howling. Oh, it was a sad, sad day. But the moon could not wipe the smile from his face. God was angry at the moon's thoughtless behavior.

It is not nice to laugh at another's misfortune. Therefore, as punishment, God does not allow the moon to shine brightly every day. Instead, the moon grows old quickly and must be born and reborn again and again and again. ༒

Noah and the Ark

A long time ago, the world was cheerful and new; the moon smiled on the mountains, great trees offered food and shelter to animals and birds, and the song of the sea was sweet. There were few people then, and they behaved themselves nicely, happy to be living in such a beautiful place.

As more and more sons and daughters were born, this new world became noisy and unruly. There was trouble everywhere. People could not learn to get along with each other. The Lord was very sad to see this happen. He was sorry that He had created man and woman to live in His beautiful world. He said, "I will destroy all traces of people, beasts and creeping things, and birds of the air. Someday, I will try again."

Living in this troublesome world was a kind and honest man named Noah. He was a good person in all ways, and he had a nice family. The Lord told Noah to help Him begin a new world. But first the Lord gave Noah certain instructions: Noah had to build an ark, a mighty boat three stories high, with one big window and a door on the side. And then Noah must cover all the wood with black, sticky pitch, so it would not leak. In seven days, Noah and the ark must be ready to leave on a long journey.

The Lord said, "I shall make a great flood and every thing that is in the earth shall perish. However, I shall make an agreement with you, Noah. You shall come into the ark with your whole family. Also, I want you to bring two of every living thing, male and female, and keep them safe with you. Make sure to gather enough food to feed yourselves and the animals, the birds, and creeping things. Hurry Noah! In seven days the rain will begin. I will cause it to rain for forty days and forty nights."

Noah followed these directions carefully and soon was ready to go.

On the seventh day, just as the Lord promised, the windows of heaven opened and it rained and poured. It didn't stop. On that day, Noah's family and the animals, large and small, bugs, lizards, goats and frogs, eagles, elephants, camels and canaries, lions and baboons, and every living thing that breathed went into the ark two by two, as the Lord commanded. As the last tail entered the ark, Noah pulled a big thatched rain cover over the roof and shut the door tightly. Everyone, man and animal, bird and bug, held their breath. At that very moment the ark began to float! A great sea was beneath it, and the ark danced on the fountains of the earth.

Everything was under water: mountains and trees, great palaces and humble houses, chariots and donkey carts, and everything that had moved upon the earth and had flown through the sky. What a dark day it was! Grass and grain, olives and beans, sunflowers and rosebushes, birds' nests and beehives, tigers and turtles, spiders and lightning bugs, berries and cherries were all gone! Only Noah and all the lucky passengers in the ark were safe and dry.

For the next forty days the ark became a city full of all different types of beings. To get things organized, Noah put the lady dove in charge. She was very graceful, with silver wings and golden feathers. Her manners were perfect and she spoke quietly and gently. She called a big meeting and rules were made. Everybody had chores to do: the big creatures helped the little ones, no pushing or shoving

was allowed, polite words like "please" and "thank you" and "excuse me" were to be used, and hands, feet, and paws had to be washed before meals.

The food was wonderful, with new dishes to taste from many different places. The camels filled the water dishes, and the ants were in charge of the food cupboards. The bees passed around honey combs till they were licked clean. The goats made milk shakes as the ark went up and down over the waves. The mules carried great packs of nuts and berries, and the little quails made huge bowls of scrambled, spotted eggs. Elephants stomped their big feet to crush barley, and the monkeys used their hands to knead bread. The leopards, keeping their claws to themselves, swiftly collected salad vegetables from the gazelles and hyenas. The pelicans' pouches were wonderful fish markets, with fresh choices every day. The caterpillars were excused from helping: they were asleep in their sleeping bags waiting to become butterflies. The great lions used their wet, rough tongues to help wipe all the mouths, and the good-natured storks volunteered to lead the clean-up squad.

Since there were many stories to share, and memories to remember, there was show-and-tell every night. The sheep brought hats and cloaks dyed blue, purple, and scarlet, and trumpets made from their horns. The jackals told funny stories, a real pair of comedians. The bears gave lessons about the stars, and the spiders offered classes in web making. The chameleons put on magic shows; they changed colors and almost disappeared. And the wolves, the lambs, the goats, the calves, and the lions put on a play. They taught everyone this poem:

Be kind to creepy crawly things,
Be kind to odd-shaped things with wings.
And please don't knock the anthill down,
It took them years to build their town.
Don't run from bees, just let them be,
And let that butterfly go free.
If all of us in peace shall live,
Then kindness must be ours to give.

20

There were many lovely voices around, and so there was quite a bit of singing. The owls gave hooting concerts, the horses whinnied, the crickets hummed, the bees buzzed, the warblers warbled, and the robins sang rain songs. On special occasions, like the swans' fiftieth wedding anniversary, Noah gave a dance party. There was only one rule: No Fast Dancing! Rocking the boat was not permitted! When it grew quiet and bedtime finally came, everyone except the wide-eyed snakes, who kept watch at night, closed their eyes and dreamed of dry land and sunny days.

The Lord remembered Noah and all the passengers in the ark. God made a great wind to blow and the windows of heaven closed. There were no more tears. The flood waters retreated and became oceans, rivers, lakes, and swimming pools. Soon the mountains stuck their tops out to dry in the warm air. At the end of forty days Noah opened the ark's big window. First, he sent a raven to look for dry land. Now a raven is very smart; it can figure things out. But it went to and fro, to and fro, and came back with no good news.

The lady dove was sent out next, but the poor bird flew around so much that its wings got tired. She could find no rest for the soles of her feet. Noah put out his hand and tenderly brought her back into the ark. After another seven days, he again sent the dove out to search for dry land. At twilight, just as Noah was about to lose hope, the dove returned. Her silver wings shimmered, her golden feathers sparkled with sunbeams, and she held a new, green olive branch in her mouth. Noah knew that if he had patience, they would soon be able to leave the ark.

After another seven days, he again sent the dove out, and she returned no more. Noah thought, "Perhaps she has found a tree to live in! Maybe the flood is finally over!" Full of happiness, Noah removed the covering of the ark and saw that the ground was dry!

The Lord spoke to Noah and said, "You may now take your family and leave the ark. Bring all the animals, the birds, and creeping things. Tell them to fill the earth and begin to make their own families."

Noah said, "Thank you very much from all of us."

The Lord was pleased. He said, "From now on, there will always be planting time and harvest time, cold and heat, the seasons shall change, and day and night shall not cease." The Lord blessed Noah and said, "Be fruitful and multiply; fill the earth with people. I promise never again to bring a great flood to destroy all living things. I will set my rainbow in the clouds. After a rain, look up at the sky. You will see My promise of a sunny day to come."

Noah, his children and their wives, and all the living creatures, the birds of the air, the cattle and every beast of the earth, and every creeping thing that had lived so nicely together, marched out of the ark, through the rainbow, into a beautiful new world.

The Tower of Babel

hen the world was young, the Lord God kept a close watch over His new people. When they traveled, He made sure they stayed together in one group. He had them speak only one language; it was important to understand directions correctly. After one of their long trips, this large group found a nice place to stay. It was good farmland, wide and green, with smooth soil. Because there were no big stones to dig out for building, the people invented bricks. Here is how they were made:

1. Take some soil that has clay in it.
2. Add water till it gets slippery.
3. Add chopped-up straw to hold it together.
4. Form into brick shapes.
5. Lay them in a sunny place to dry.
6. After drying, put the bricks in a hot oven for several days.
7. Let them cool slowly in the same oven.
8. Remove the cool bricks from the oven and start building.

Now that they had bricks, the new people said, "Come let us build a city, and a tower, with its top in heaven. We shall all stay together and make a great name for ourselves." They thought that if their tower reached up into God's heaven, this would make them also mighty and honored. But this was a selfish goal. They forgot that they were God's creation; nobody was supposed to be greater than God.

One day, God came down to take a look at the city and the tower. He did not like what He saw! He said, "Here are one people with one language and they should be living peacefully, enjoying their beautiful new world. But what do they do? They try to build

a tower that will reach up to My heaven! I must stop the building of this tower! I think these people are growing too high and mighty. They are trying to be like their Creator and rule the world. Since I created the world, I am the only ruler allowed. I shall confuse them by making them all speak different languages. This way they will not be able to understand one another and this tower-building will stop! They will no longer live together because I shall scatter them over the face of the earth. They will become different nationalities of people and will have to work hard to keep peace in the world!"

High up in the tower, the people started arguing with each other. There was such a racket! But since nobody could understand what the other was saying, all work stopped. The city and its tower were never finished. The people, babbling together in groups, scattered all over the face of the earth. In this way, the Lord caused something good to come out of something bad: He created all the new languages for the new countries in His new young world.

The Story of Abraham

For many years after Noah, God tried to teach His new people the correct way of life. He kept trying for ten generations. That's a long time. But there were so many people, and as they grew wealthy and strong, they forgot the ways of God. They wouldn't listen and became wild and unruly. Worst of all, they began to worship statues made of wood and stone. These were called idols. When God saw this, He was angry!

"I have an idea," He thought. "I'll give it one more try. Tonight, a baby will be born into the house of Terach and they will name him Abram. Although all babies are wonderful to Me, this child will be special. I will make him a great leader, one who will love God and teach these people to behave. He shall become the father of a great nation."

And so Abram, the great-great-great-great-great-great-great-great-grandson of Noah, was born. On that warm, moonlit night, millions of stars gave light to his eyes, a sweet scent of perfume filled the air, and the song of God rocked him to sleep.

Abram's Early Life

God watched over Abram as he grew up. He saw that Abram was kind to animals—he spoke softly to the sheep and the goats, and they obeyed his orders and came home on time. He was a good son and sometimes helped out by working in his father's idol shop, although he had his own opinions about such things. He tried hard to make the others, including his father, understand that there was only one God to worship. But he was still just a boy and older people don't often listen to younger people—although sometimes it would be a good thing to do.

When Abram became a handsome young man, he married a beautiful woman named Sarai. Their wedding was lovely. The tents were all decorated with flowers and tinkling bells. The guests sat on handwoven rugs and ate delicious food. When the band started clanging their cymbals, everyone got up and danced. Sarai and Abram were a lovely bride and groom.

Soon after the wedding, Abram's father, Terach, decided that it was time to move to a bigger city. In those days, families lived and traveled together. Abram and Sarai and the rest of the family, including Abram's nephew Lot, gathered together the sheep and the goats, the tents, rugs, pots, pans, pitchers, and water jugs, blankets, dishes, donkey carts, doll carriages, kickballs, and the pet fish (which they carried in a blue bowl). Off they went to live in Haran, a crowded town where

The camel trains stopped
And everyone shopped
For bracelets and beads,
And black poppy seeds.
The salt seller was busy,
His sales made him dizzy.
Like bees with their honey,
These people made money!

It was an easy life but maybe not such a good life. Having lots of nice things does not always bring happiness.

Terach lived to be an old man. After he died Abram was sad. God thought that this would be the right time to call Abram and explain what his future job was to be. When you are sad it's good to get started on a new project. This can help you feel better.

God said, "You must leave this rich country, your friends, and your father's nice house and go into this land that I have chosen for you. I will make you and your people into a great nation. I will bless you and make your name great so that your name will be a blessing. I will bless them who bless you and curse them who curse you. You shall teach all the people on earth about My existence, and they too, shall be blessed."

Because Abram trusted God, he was not afraid to leave home and journey to a strange land. And since it is nice to share good things with others, Abram was happy with his mission: to share the blessing of his knowledge of God.

Abram and Lot

Abram was a good leader. Many people followed along with his family as they left to go to Canaan, their new land. You see, Abram had a good reputation.

1. He was friendly and always invited new people for dinner. Of course, he was lucky that Sarai, his wife, was such a good cook. She made honey cake, cherry blintzes, fruit salad, and the best goat's milk shakes ever. Everyone loved coming to Abram's tent; it was always a meal to remember. After eating, they thanked God for their good fortune. Without God there would be

No sun and rain,
No land and no seeds,
No cows, goats, and sheep
And no people to feed.

2. He was charitable and helped the needy: Abram never passed a beggar without giving a coin; after all, except for the kindness of God, he too could be poor.

3. He was always fair: It is important to understand both sides

of a problem. Abram believed that all men and women were brothers and sisters. Even if some behaved poorly, Abram tried very hard to find something to like about them. And he always tried to say something nice.

When Abram's family and friends reached Canaan, they settled in Shechem, a place where workers worked hard and helped each other. Abram thought this would be a good example for his own group. It must have been the right choice because God appeared to Abram and said, "I will give this land to your children." In this beautiful spot, Abram built an altar, a place where, in those days, an animal would be roasted and offered to God as a way of thanks. This way, if it didn't rain enough for the crops to grow, and he had to pack up and leave in order to find food, the altar would be there, waiting, when he returned. He would know he was home.

After a short trip to Egypt, for just this very reason, Abram and his family and friends and goats and sheep came back and found their altar. They unpacked the tents, the rugs, the pots, pans, pitchers, and water jugs, blankets, dishes, donkey carts, doll carriages, kickballs, and the pet fish (which they carried in a blue bowl). By this time, Abram had become a rich man. He had silver and gold, servants and camels, and Sarai had gorgeous silk dresses and two sets of dishes. Lot, too, had become wealthy. He had rugs and blankets, and tents with curtains, a nice big soup pot, goats and sheep, and herds of cattle, cattle herders, sheep shepherds, goat milkers, dirt diggers, and camel riders. Everybody had everything and this became a big problem. There were too many people living and working in one spot. And you know what happens when that happens:

Fighting and biting,
Yelling and screaming,
Hitting and quitting,
And pushing and shoving.
Arguments over the smallest of spaces,
No smiles on their faces,
They forgot about loving.

Abram, who loved his nephew Lot, did not want any more trouble between the workers. He saw that there was not enough room for everyone. Because he was a thoughtful man, Abram said to Lot, "We are one people and should not fight. There is a whole land before us. Let us separate. If you take the land by my left hand, I will go to the right. If you take the land by my right hand, I will go to the left."

Abram gave Lot the first choice. That was very fair. In order to live peacefully, sometimes we must give more than our share, especially to those closest to us. Lot looked around and saw a big area with rich soil and green, well-watered fields. "It's like the Garden of Eden," he thought, and quickly chose this site.

Just because something is pretty does not always mean it's the best. Abram saw the whole world as a beautiful gift from God. He was content with what was left for him, even though the land was rocky and hilly and sea breezes blew salt air. But he missed his nephew Lot. It is hard to live away from your family.

God saw that Abram was sad once more and thought that this would be a good time for another visit. He said, "Lift up your eyes and look around you, northward and southward, eastward and westward. All the land that you see I will give you, and to your children, and your children's children forevermore. If you can number all the pieces of dust in the earth, that's how many people shall follow you. Arise and walk through the land. It is yours."

Abram moved his family, his servants, and his friends, his gold and silver that he kept in a carved, wooden chest, the sheep, goats, and camels, the tents, rugs, pots, pans, pitchers, and water jugs, the blankets and pillows, the everyday dishes and the good set of dishes, the new wine goblets and Sarai's beautiful silk dresses, the donkey carts, doll carriages, kickballs, and the pet fish (which they carried in a blue bowl) and walked through his new land as God had commanded. When he finally stopped, he built another altar as thanks to God.

THANK YOU PRAYER

Thank you, God, for this wonderful land.
Thank you, God, for caring.
Thank you, God, for your helping hand.
We'll thank you, God, by sharing.
A little bit here, a little bit there,
Growing vegetables, fruit, and wheat,
We'll farm the fields and milk the goats,
There'll be plenty for all to eat.
Thank you, God, for the morning sun.
Thank you, God, for sharing
Your seeds and water, your starlit skies,
We'll thank you, God, by caring.

Abram Becomes Abraham

Abram's nephew, Lot, had been living just outside the walls of the city of Sodom. He had many tents; there was one for cooking, one for sleeping, one for eating, one for bathing, and one for entertaining company, with fancy rugs and big, stuffed pillows. Outside, his herds of cattle, sheep, and camels happily chewed the grass and grain while his goats chewed anything they could get their teeth into. This was indeed a beautiful, green place, a nice country home. But the people of Sodom and the neighboring town, Gomorrah, were wicked. Their loud noises could be heard in heaven, and God did not like this at all. They were always having wars, fighting one king after another. Sometimes they were winners and sometimes they were losers. One time, when they were losing, their enemies took all the goods of Sodom and Gomorrah, all the food, all the men and women, and also captured Abram's nephew Lot as he sat outside his tent eating some yogurt.

When Abram heard this news, he was determined to save Lot. He took three hundred and eighteen strong men and went to the rescue. Under Abram's fine leadership, they fought hard and brought back not only Lot but the food, the goods, and all the men and women of Sodom and Gomorrah, even though, as you know, they were not nice people. The King of Sodom was grateful and offered Abram anything he wished. Abram said, "I will take not a thread or a shoelace from you. Just give me enough food for my men. However, if any of my team who shared this dangerous battle wants prizes, then that is fine with me. It's their choice." Abram knew that it is not really necessary to be rewarded for doing a good deed.

Once again, the Lord came to Abram, this time in a vision. He told Abram that He wanted to give him a reward for obeying God's call to help others. Abram said to God, "The only thing I desire is for my wife, Sarai, and I to have a child of our own. A child is the greatest of treasures, the greatest of gifts." Abram was not afraid to speak up.

The Lord said, "The child who is born to you shall be your heir. Look at the sky and count the stars. If you can count them, that will be the number of your descendants. You will have children, and grandchildren, and great-grandchildren, and great-great-grandchildren. As many greats as you can name, so great shall be your future." And Abram trusted the Lord.

When Abram was ninety-nine years old, the Lord appeared again. He said to Abram, "I am God Almighty. My promise is with you. You shall be the father of many nations. Great kings shall come from you. Your name shall no longer be Abram, but your new name shall be Abraham, which means 'Father of Many.' " God, by putting the letter "H" into Abram's name, gave him a piece of His heart. Now it was Abraham's job to carry God's heart to all the people.

Then God commanded, "Every male among you shall be circumcised. This will be the Sign of the Covenant between Me and you. And throughout the generations, every male among you shall be circumcised at the age of eight days."

And God said to Abraham, "I shall now call your wife 'Sarah,' which means 'Princess.' I shall bless her and she shall have your son. I shall bless her and she shall be the mother of nations. Great kings will someday come from her."

At this point, Abraham was so astonished that he laughed. "Can he who is one hundred years old become a father? And how can a ninety-year-old woman have a child?"

God repeated, "Sarah shall bear you a son and his name shall be Isaac."

Shortly after God spoke to Abraham, three strangers came to visit. It is not always a good idea to talk to strangers, but Abraham was a wise grown-up and he was very careful. He knew, in his heart, that these particular men were safe. Because he was polite, and a good host, Abraham insisted that they stay for a meal. "Where is your wife, Sarah?" they asked. "She is in the tent making raisin bread," said Abraham. One of the men said, "Listen to me. I shall return in a year's time and Sarah shall have a son."

Sarah, who had her ear against the tent door, laughed to herself. "How can I, such an old, old woman, have a little baby? What will my friends say?"

The Lord, Who hears everything, asked Abraham, "Why did Sarah laugh? She should know that nothing is too impossible for the Lord to do. Sarah shall have a son!"

When asked about it, Sarah denied that she had laughed. She felt guilty about her impolite eavesdropping and was afraid to tell the truth. But God, Who is very understanding, said gently, "No, Sarah, I heard you laugh. But don't worry. You shall have a son and his name shall be 'Isaac, Child of Laughter.'"

Soon Sarah was sewing baby clothes, weaving blankets, and practicing lullabies. A lovely smile came to Sarah's face, and once in a while she would feel just like a young girl and dance round and round in a circle of joy.

Sodom and Gomorrah

Soon after the Lord made the wonderful promise of a child to Abraham and Sarah, He had to take care of a different kind of problem, one that would not have such a happy ending. The Lord had heard awful stories about the towns of Sodom and Gomorrah. The people who lived there were selfish and nasty. They had become rich and greedy and had forgotten their simple upbringing. They pretended to be nice, stole from each other, lied, and were rude and mean to strangers. These stories made the Lord angry. One day He said to Abraham, "This is a very bad group. I shall come down and investigate and see if they are as bad as they look from up here. If they are, I shall have to destroy them!"

Abraham, who was kind and just, had sympathy for these people. He felt that all men were his brothers, all women, his sisters. He tried very hard to bargain with God. He said, "Would You sweep away the good with the wicked? How about if there are fifty good people? Will You spare this place for the sake of fifty good men and women? The Judge of the Earth must act justly."

The Lord answered, "If I find fifty good people within the cities, I will forgive the entire place."

Abraham was brave. He again dared to speak up to the Lord. "What if there are forty-five good people? Will You destroy the cities for five people less than fifty?"

And the Lord replied, "I will not destroy them if I find forty-five good people there."

Then Abraham said, "How about forty good people?"

The Lord answered, "I will not do it."

"How about thirty?" asked Abraham.

"I will not do it," said the Lord.

Then Abraham said, "Please don't be angry, Lord, but what if You find ten good people?"

"I will not destroy the cities for the sake of ten good people," said the Lord.

But after all this bargaining, and despite all of Abraham's hard work, the Lord could find no good people in the cities of Sodom and Gomorrah. Sometimes, no matter how hard you try, things don't work out. However, there was one happy bit of news: since Lot and his family lived outside the walls of the city of Sodom, God decided to save them.

Lot enjoyed relaxing in his entertainment tent. He would lean back on his pillows, have a nice glass of cold goat's milk, and read the latest clay tablets. One day, two angels, dressed as regular men, knocked on the tent door. Lot was hospitable, like his uncle Abraham. He welcomed the men and politely asked them to wipe the sand from their feet before stepping on his new rugs. He warned them, for their own protection, not to go into the city of Sodom, but to stay with him. Lot then went out and begged the townspeople, who had gathered like wild beasts at the sight of strangers, to go away. The angels pulled him back inside the tent and told Lot that the two cities and all the nasty people were to be destroyed. They asked if Lot had any decent relatives that he would like to save. Naturally, he would save his wife and daughters, but what about his daughters' husbands? Lot found his sons-in-law and told them what was about to happen. They thought it was a big joke, and they went back into the town of Sodom to join their friends.

As the sun came up over the beautiful green hills, the angels told Lot, "Hurry, take your wife and your two daughters. Otherwise they will be swept away!"

For just a second Lot hesitated. But God had pity for him. He thought, "I know that Lot is a good man, even though he doubts Me." He brought him outside and the angels shouted, "Escape for your life and do not look back! Go up to the mountains! Quickly!"

Lot was shaking in his sandals; he was afraid of heights. "I am not a good climber," he said. "Can't I please go to a nearby town?"

God, Who had great patience, said, "All right, but hurry!" He couldn't destroy Sodom and Gomorrah until Lot was safe.

Lot's wife was also told not to look back and only to look forward to a new life. But she missed her nasty, rude, greedy, friends. She disobeyed orders and looked back. Immediately she turned into a pillar of salt. In the old days, Lot's wife had been so selfish that she had even refused to share her own salt. Now, in spite of herself, she became unselfish. Forevermore, all the creatures who lived on earth, the people, animals, birds, and bugs, could take as much salt as they wished from her.

Abraham and Isaac

A child is a gift from God—the greatest gift. A child's first sweet cry fills the air with music; its first sweet smile brightens the world. Abraham's world was very bright. His new son, Isaac, made the old man feel young again. They took long walks together in the hills looking for butterflies and beehives. They took donkey rides across the desert and went swimming in water holes. Isaac told Abraham funny stories about his teachers at school, and Abraham told Isaac what it was like in the old days. Abraham would say, "Now in my day . . ." and Isaac would say, "Oh, Father, not that story again." Abraham would continue and they would both laugh. They were good friends. As Isaac grew older, Abraham carefully taught him the ways of God.

THE WAYS OF GOD

Be brave when your knees are shaking,
Be kind, there's no need to be cruel,
Be faithful and loving,

Honest and fair,
Learn to listen and follow the rules.
Respect someone else's opinions,
Though they may seem silly or odd,
Feel free to ask questions,
Be thoughtful and wise,
These are the ways of God.

One day, God tested Abraham's faith and love.

"Abraham," He said.

"I am here," Abraham answered, always ready to do as God might wish.

God said, "Take your son, your one and only son, whom you love so dearly, to the land of Moriah. There, on top of a special mountain, you must offer Isaac as a burnt offering."

At first, Abraham must have been terribly upset. What was God's reason for asking him to do such a dreadful thing? His people did not offer human sacrifices. A child is a precious gift from God. Why would God want to take this gift away? Abraham asked himself these questions over and over. Deep in his heart, his heart that was full of the knowledge of God, he knew that God would provide the answer if he trusted Him. This still did not make things any easier for Abraham: He did not want to frighten his son. Isaac was still learning the ways of God.

At dawn, Abraham put a saddle on his donkey. He did not waste time; he was obeying God. He took two young helpers along with his son Isaac. But he cut the wood himself because this was to be his own very special offering. After three days of travel, Abraham looked up and saw the place on the mountain that God had chosen. It was far off, high in the clouds, and lit by a mysterious light that only Abraham could see. He told his helpers to wait for him, that he and his son would come back after they worshiped. Perhaps, in his heart of hearts, Abraham felt that he might return with Isaac. But was God's will to be doubted?

Abraham took the bundle of wood and placed it upon Isaac's back. The child never complained. He was a good son and was used to helping his father. Abraham carried the sharp, shiny knife and the container of coals to light the fire. Abraham led Isaac up the mountain. Step by step they went together, father and son, just as they always had done. But Abraham was quiet. He didn't whistle back to the birds. He didn't point out different animal tracks. He didn't tell Isaac to gather berries for a snack. And Isaac, who was following along, kicking pebbles and collecting leaves, began to worry. Why was his wonderful father behaving so strangely? Why was he so silent?

"My father," said Isaac.

Abraham replied, "I am here, my son."

And Isaac, a curious lad who felt free to ask questions, asked, "Here is the fire and the wood; but where is the lamb for the burnt offering?"

Abraham said, "God will provide Himself the lamb for a burnt offering, my son."

By now, Isaac was frightened inside. But he was determined to have courage. Though he was young, he had learned many of the ways of God. He understood that something important was about to happen, something awesome. Isaac trusted his father, just as Abraham trusted God.

Together they went to the place that God had chosen. Abraham built the altar and carefully put the wood down. As gently as he could, he tied a strong rope around Isaac and laid him upon the wood. The old steady heart of Abraham and the young sturdy heart of Isaac beat together calmly, and with love. Abraham then stretched out his hand and raised the sharp, shiny knife to slay his son.

At the very next moment, right before it was almost too late, the angel who spoke for God called to him from heaven, "Abraham, Abraham!"

Abraham answered, "I am here."

And the angel said, "Do not lay your hand upon the lad, do not hurt him; for now I know you are a God-fearing man since you have not held back your son, your only son, from Me."

Abraham, looking up, saw a ram caught by his horns in some

bushes. It must have been there all the time. Isaac, who had been holding his breath, let out a big sigh of relief. Quickly, Abraham untied his son, who jumped off the altar as fast as he could. Then Abraham took the ram, prepared it, and sacrificed it instead of Isaac. He named this sacred spot "The Place Where the Lord is Seen." He sees and is seen, not in the eyes but in the heart.

The angel of the Lord called out to Abraham a second time and said, "Since you have not held back your son, your only son, whom you love so dearly, I will bless you and multiply your people as the stars of the heaven and as the sand on the seashore. Your people will capture their enemies and, because of you, all the nations of earth will be blessed. This is because you have listened to God."

The ways of God are sometimes difficult to understand. But if you trust in God and have courage and faith, especially when it seems that all hope is lost, then wonderful miracles can happen. Abraham loved God and had faith. Isaac was brave and trusting. With grateful hearts, father and son began the long walk down the mountain—Isaac, happy and relieved, in the lead, Abraham, content to be a bit slower, a step behind. Isaac stopped to let Abraham catch up to him, and they both started hugging and kissing and laughing and crying at the same time. With their arms around each other, Abraham and Isaac walked together into their glorious, God-given future.

Isaac and Rebekah

Abraham, Sarah, and their son, Isaac, lived in Canaan, the land promised to them by God. Isaac took care of the animals, Abraham grew tomatoes, eggplant, and string beans, and Sarah baked wonderful bread in the oven behind their big tent. They were good neighbors and their camels were well behaved. Their home was a fine place to visit. It had green plants in hanging pots, colorful rugs, big, soft pillows, and two singing birds in a silver cage. People were always dropping by to say hello and Abraham thanked God for his happy life.

When Sarah reached the age of one hundred and twenty-seven years, God called her to heaven. Abraham and Isaac were sad. It was hard to say good-bye forever to someone they loved. But lovely memories make heavy hearts lighter, and Abraham and Isaac, when they remembered all the nice things about their wife and mother, soon were feeling a little better. However, there was one big problem: the tent felt empty. The Sabbath candles no longer made dancing shadows on the walls, the smell of fresh bread baking was gone, and there were no more dinner parties. Father and son were lonely. It was very quiet; even the singing birds in their silver cage were silent.

Abraham had an idea: perhaps this might be the right time to find a wife for Isaac.

In those faraway days, it was common for a father to seek a wife for his son. Abraham said to his chief servant, Eliezer, "I want you to find a wife for my son Isaac. But I do not want her to be a daughter of the Canaanites. They still worship idols and do some pretty bad things. Go back to my old country and my relatives, and find a wife for Isaac."

The servant, Eliezer, said, "What if the woman refuses to follow me? Should I then take Isaac back to your old country?"

Abraham answered, "Whatever you do, don't take Isaac back there with you." Abraham did not want Isaac to leave this Promised Land. He knew he had to stay and fulfill God's command to give the land to his children. If Isaac left, all would be lost. Abraham told the servant that God would be sending an angel along on the journey to protect him. "Good luck, Eliezer, and come back soon," said Abraham, waving good-bye.

Eliezer the servant took ten camels and departed. He also packed many nice things: gold and silver bracelets, nose rings and earrings, a goatskin belt, a white wool coat, two strings of tinkling bells, and a beaded dance dress in rainbow colors. When Eliezer arrived outside the gates of Abraham's old town, he prayed to the Lord, "Oh Lord, God of my master Abraham, give me good luck today. I will stand by this well where the young women come to draw water. If the maiden whom I ask for a drink answers, 'Drink, and I shall also give your camels something to drink,' I will know that she's the one that You have chosen for my master, Abraham."

No sooner said than done! As he was praying, a young woman with long, dark hair came walking down toward the well. After filling her water pitcher, she put it on her shoulder and began to walk away. The servant, who could hardly believe his instant good luck, said, "Please give me a little water to drink from your pitcher."

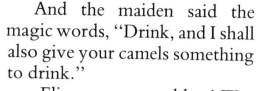

And the maiden said the magic words, "Drink, and I shall also give your camels something to drink."

Eliezer was speechless! Was this the right girl? So soon? "Well," he thought, "she is kind to animals, polite to strangers, and very good looking." He waited till the camels had their drink and then took out a golden ring and two silver bracelets. He offered them to the girl and asked, "Whose daughter are you?"

The girl answered, "I am Rebekah, the daughter of Bethuel, the son of Milcah." These were Abraham's relatives! And just like Abraham, Rebekah was gracious and hospitable. She said, "We have food for your camels and extra rooms for you and your camel riders. Come and stay with us." Eliezer bowed his head and thanked God for having led him in the right direction.

Rebekah ran home and showed the golden ring and the silver bracelets to her brother, Laban. He came back to the fountain and greeted Eliezer. "Come into my house," he said. "Don't stand outside. There's plenty of room and food for all."

Eliezer and his camel riders came to the house and fed the hungry animals. Then they washed the sand from their own feet. This was very good manners. As they entered Rebekah's house, all kinds of delicious food awaited them:

There was cucumber salad
With onions and dill,
Falafel and pita
Fresh from the grill,
Eggplant and tomatoes,
Chickpeas and stew,
Carrots with honey
And chicken soup too.

Eliezer said, "I will not eat till I tell you why I am here."

"Speak," said Laban.

"I am Abraham's servant," he said, "and the Lord has blessed him greatly. He has given him flocks and herds, silver and gold, menservants and maidservants, and camels and donkeys. His wife, Sarah, blessed him with a son when she was old; and he has given all his wealth and blessings to this son, who is named Isaac. My master told me to go back to the land where he was born and find a wife for his son. He sent an angel of the Lord to help me. And when I came to this well, I prayed to the Lord and said, 'Let it come to pass that if the maid whom I ask for a drink answers me, "Drink, and I shall also fetch water for your camels," then I will know that this is the right woman for my master's son.' And what do you know! No sooner said than done! There was Rebekah, walking down to the well! I said, 'Please give me a little water to drink from your pitcher.' She put down the pitcher and said the magic words, 'Drink, and I shall also fetch water for your camels.' She's the one! Now, will you deal kindly with my master and allow Rebekah to become Isaac's wife?"

Laban and Bethuel answered, "This is the Lord's doing and we will not go against it. Here is Rebekah. Take her to be your master's wife."

First, the servant bowed down in thanks to God. Then he gave wonderful gifts to the family: Rebekah received jewels of silver and jewels of gold, nose rings and earrings, and the beaded dance dress in rainbow colors. Her brother, Laban, was given the goatskin belt. The white wool coat fit Rebekah's mother perfectly, and her father, Bethuel, couldn't wait to attach the tinkling bells to the front door.

There are many kinds of gifts: A drink of water can be as much a gift to a thirsty person as a precious jewel is to a young bride. A promise is a gift, and a surprise is an especially wonderful gift. All gifts are nice because someone was thoughtful enough to give them and, of course, someone else was respectful enough to say thank you. Rebekah's family thanked Eliezer over and over, and then everyone sat down to a great feast. Soon all were asleep; the camel riders were snoring, and the camels were snorting. It had been a good day.

In the morning, Eliezer the servant was up early, ready to go home. But Rebekah's brother and her mother were reluctant to see her leave. They said, "Let her stay just a little longer. Then she can go."

The servant answered, "Since the Lord has helped me to find Rebekah, you must not delay me. Let me return to my master."

Rebekah's family said, "Then we shall call her and ask if she is willing." No woman could be given in marriage against her wishes. This was a strict rule.

"Will you go with this man?" they asked.

"I will go," said Rebekah. She had a good feeling about this decision. Sometimes you just know.

Her family blessed Rebekah and said, "May you become the mother of tens of thousands." They hugged and kissed and said good-bye. Rebekah packed all of her belongings:

Sandals and a sundial,
To know when to wake up,
Bracelets a brush and a comb,
Candlesticks, breadboards,
The lovely new gifts,
And her favorite old doll
To remind her of home.

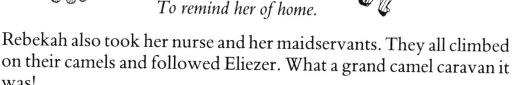

Rebekah also took her nurse and her maidservants. They all climbed on their camels and followed Eliezer. What a grand camel caravan it was!

Isaac was having some quiet time alone in one of his fields. He looked up and saw camels. "Camels?" he thought. "Who in the world is coming?"

From high up on her camel, Rebekah saw Isaac. She jumped down and said to the servant, "Who is that man walking over to meet us?" Her heart was pounding.

"It is Isaac, my master," said Eliezer.

Rebekah, smiling, pulled her veil over her eyes while the servant told Isaac all that had happened. Isaac could not believe his eyes. He looked and looked at Rebekah. It was love at first sight! Rebekah felt exactly the same way. Sometimes you just know.

After introducing his bride to his father, Isaac and Rebekah went to their tent and became husband and wife. Soon the Sabbath candles made dancing shadows on the tent walls, the wonderful smell of bread baking filled the air, visitors stayed for dinner, and the singing birds in their silver cage once again sang cheerful songs. Abraham's tent no longer felt empty. It was full of love.

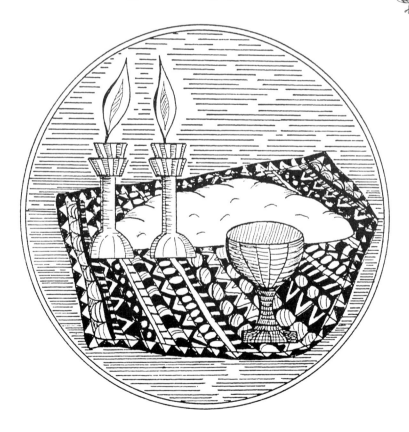

Jacob and Esau

Did you know that no two people in the world are alike? You could go from here to the moon and never see anyone exactly like you. Everyone is different, even twins. Some twins are "identical," that is, they look almost exactly alike. But once you get to know them, you can spot all sorts of differences. "Fraternal" twins sometimes do not look at all alike, even though they were born together, one after the other. The important thing to remember about twins is: all people, whether they look somewhat alike or not, have very different personalities.

SOME PEOPLE

Some people are lazy,
Some people work hard,
Some behave better than others,
Some people sleep late,
Others won't go to bed,
And some people fight with their brothers.

Some people are quiet,
And others talk loud,
Some have straight teeth,
And others wear braces,
Some people pout,
And some people frown,
But most people have smiles on their faces.

After many years, Isaac and Rebekah were blessed with a set of twins. Before they were born, the Lord said to Rebekah:

"Two nations are in your body,
And two people shall be separated from you;
The one people shall be stronger than the other people;
And the older shall serve the younger."

In those days, the oldest or firstborn son was given what was called "The Birthright." Great responsibilities came with this honor:

1. He was in charge of leading family prayers. This was a very special job that required much studying.
2. He would receive the largest share of the family possessions.
3. He was supposed to have good sense and play fair.
4. He was expected to take care of his younger brothers and sisters.

However, the Lord told Rebekah that just the opposite would happen: "The older shall serve the younger."

When nine months were over, Rebekah gave birth to fraternal twins. The first one was red-faced and was covered with hair. They called him Esau. When the second one came, he was holding on to his brother's heel. He could hardly wait to be born! They called him Jacob. These brothers had very different personalities. As they grew up they would fight and make up and then fight again. Just because they were brothers did not mean that they would always get along. Esau chased the animals around the farm and Jacob would try to keep them as pets. Esau would sing and make noise while Jacob was trying to do his homework. Esau was bored with prayers. He liked being outdoors, camping and hunting, and he would bring back just the kind of meat that his father Isaac enjoyed. Because of this, he soon became his father's favorite son. Jacob was quiet. He helped his mother around the tent and was very good at learning prayers and reading stories. He was gentle and kind and soon became his mother's favorite.

It is not wise for parents to have a favorite child; most parents love their children equally. However, nobody is perfect. Isaac and Rebekah had lived a long time before having children. They each had their own ideas about what was important in life, and they did not agree on how to raise their sons.

One day, Jacob was making lentil stew, a spicy dish that smelled wonderful. Esau came in from the field and said, "Please let me eat some of this lentil stew. I am so hungry, I could faint."

Jacob, who was very clever, said, "First sell me your birthright."

And Esau said, "I feel like I am dying from hunger, so what good will my birthright do me?"

Jacob said, "Give me your word."

Esau gave him his word and sold his birthright to Jacob. Esau did not think about what he was doing; the food smelled delicious and all he wanted to do was eat. Jacob gave his brother bread and stew and Esau ate until he was stuffed. Since he had no interest in anything but his own pleasures, Esau traded away his birthright, and the honor that came with it, for a full stomach.

Jacob's Blessing

When Isaac grew old, his eyes were so dim he could hardly see. He called Esau, his older son, and said to him, "My son."

Esau replied, "I am here."

Isaac said, "As you can see, I am old and do not know how soon I will die. Please take your bow and arrows out to the field and bring home some tasty meat. Then make a delicious dish, one that I really love, and bring it to me for dinner. Afterward, I shall give you my blessing." It was the father's duty to give his special blessing to the firstborn son. Isaac had no idea that Esau had sold his birthright to Jacob for a meal of lentil stew.

Rebekah had her ear to the tent wall. Although she should not have been listening to a private conversation, she remembered what the Lord had told her so many years ago: "The elder shall serve the younger." Because she was the mother, she felt that she knew what was really best for the family. You see, Esau was not a good leader or a religious man. It would be a mistake for Isaac to give him the special blessing. Esau would not care about the promise that God made to their grandfather Abraham. The whole family's future and that of a nation blessed by God would be in danger! And so Rebekah devised a clever way to help this situation.

Rebekah said to Jacob, "I overheard your father speaking to Esau. He asked him to hunt some meat and make him a delicious meal. Afterward, he is going to give him his blessing. Now listen, Jacob, do as I say. Go out to the farmyard and get me two young goats. I will make a wonderful dish for your father, one that he really loves. And you shall bring it to your father to eat. This way he will bless you before his death."

Jacob said to his mother, "But my brother Esau is a hairy man and I am a not. What if my father, who can't see well, touches me? He will know that he has been tricked. I shall bring a curse upon myself, not a blessing."

His mother said, "I will take care of this hairy problem. And if anything happens to you, I will take the blame. Just listen to me and get those goats!"

And so Jacob brought the goats to Rebekah and she made delicious food for her husband. Then she took some of Esau's clothes and put them on Jacob. She wrapped the hairy skin from the goats around Jacob's hands and neck, put the food on a nice tray, and sent him in to Isaac.

"My father," said Jacob.

Isaac answered, "Who are you, my son?"

And Jacob said to his father, "I am Esau, your firstborn son. I have done as you wished. Please sit up and eat my delicious meal so that you may bless me afterward."

Isaac had not expected his dinner to arrive quite so soon. "How did you find this food so quickly, my son?" he asked with curiosity.

Jacob, thinking fast, said, "Because the Lord your God gave me good luck."

Isaac was still not sure. Esau was not a religious man and it was strange to hear him talk about God. "Come near, please, so that I may touch you, to make sure that you really are Esau, my firstborn son," Isaac said, reaching out. When he felt Jacob he said, "The voice is the voice of Jacob but the hands are the hands of Esau."

The goat hair trick had worked! Isaac told his son to bring the food closer so that he could eat. He ate a fine dinner of roast goat, chicken noodle soup, blackberry wine, and honey cake for dessert. After he finished, Isaac wiped his mouth and said, "Come near now and kiss me, my son." When Isaac smelled Esau's clothing on Jacob he said:

"See, the smell of my son
Is like the smell of a field that the Lord has blessed.
So may God give you the dew from heaven,
And good land to grow crops,
And plenty of grain and wine.
Let people serve you,
And nations bow down to you.
Take care of your fellow men and women,
And your brothers will listen to you and give you respect."

Right after Isaac finished blessing Jacob, and Jacob had left the room, Esau came back from hunting. He had prepared the tasty meal that his father had requested. Carrying it in to Isaac he said, "Please father, sit up and eat my delicious food and then give me your blessing."

Isaac said, "Who are you?"

And he answered, "I am your son, your firstborn son, Esau."

"Who came in before you and brought me roast goat and chicken noodle soup, blackberry wine and honeycake? It was certainly a wonderful meal! I ate it all up and gave him my blessing and he shall be blessed!" said Isaac, becoming upset.

Esau began to cry loudly. Bitter tears poured down his cheeks.

60

"My brother Jacob tricked you," he sobbed. "This is the second time he has taken something from me." Esau did not mention that he had actually sold his birthright to Jacob for a pot of stew. He wanted to blame everything on his brother. "Haven't you saved a blessing for me, father?" he cried.

Isaac replied, "I have made Jacob your leader and have given him servants and possessions. What shall I do for you, my son?"

"Do you only have one blessing? Bless me too, my father," said this strong man, crying like a little child.

This made Isaac feel terrible. Parents become sad when their children are unhappy. After some thought, Isaac found a blessing for Esau. He said:

"You shall live outdoors where the land is good,
Where the dew from heaven helps water the crops.
You shall fight with a sword and obey your brother.
Someday, you will leave
And break away from your brother's rule."

Esau was very angry at Jacob. He said, "After my father's death, I shall kill my brother!"

When Rebekah learned about this she quickly thought of another way to help Jacob. One trick sometimes leads to another. She told Jacob about Esau's terrible plans. "Now listen to me, my son. You must get away from here. I will arrange it so that your father sends you to my brother Laban's house in the old country. Stay with him till Esau gets over being angry. Then I will send for you."

Rebekah then went to see Isaac. She said, "I am tired of all the women around here. They are not very friendly and do not follow our traditions. If Jacob marries one of them, all will be lost." She hoped her husband would remember that his parents, Abraham and Sarah, had sent him back to his relatives to find a wife. Smiling, she remembered how they had met, so many years ago. If she were lucky, he would send Jacob out to do the same. And that is exactly what he did.

Again, Rebekah knew what was right for her family. Isaac sent Jacob away to find a wife in the land of his ancestors. He said, "May God Almighty bless you and make you fruitful and multiply and become a mighty nation. May the blessing of Abraham go with you."

Rebekah helped Jacob pack his bags and load up his camels. She had saved him some dinner, and this she tucked into his saddlebag along with a soft pillow and a warm, wool blanket. "Good-bye, Mother," called Jacob from high up on the animal's hump. Rebekah took out her handkerchief and wiped her eyes. She was sad to see her son leave but felt relieved that he would be safe. Mothers cry for many different reasons:

Mothers cry when they're happy,
And cry when they're sad,
They cry when they're proud
And cry when they're mad.
Mothers cry the first time
That their own baby cries,
And they cry when their children
Say their good-byes.

Jacob's Dream

It was not easy to travel in Jacob's time. The roads were full of rocks and holes and riding a camel was a bumpy adventure. Camels do not always want to cooperate; when they feel like stopping they lie down, and nothing can make them get up. After a long day's ride, Jacob looked for a rest stop before his camels found one for him. Along the road there were places left by other travelers, with stones piled up for tables and benches. Jacob found a sheltered area, climbed down from his high perch, fed the camels, then sat at one of the tables and had his own dinner. As it grew dark, and the first star winked in the sky, Jacob said his prayers. Then he found a nice, smooth stone for a headrest. Sleep closed his eyes, and he dreamed a marvelous dream.

JACOB'S DREAM

A ladder of flowers,
Its top reaching high,
Into the clouds,
Into the sky.

63

Angels were climbing,
On delicate toes,
One step at a time
Trailing ribbons and bows.
God heard them singing,
Their sweet voices ringing
With praises and prayers
As they climbed up the stairs.
One step at a time,
With moonbeams for light,
Into the clouds,
Into the night,
The angels touched heaven,
A long, winding line,
Then they climbed down the ladder
One step at a time,
Into the sun,
Trailing ribbons and bows,
Bringing greetings from God
To the people below.

In this wonderful dream, the Lord stood beside Jacob and said, "I am the Lord, the God of Abraham, your grandfather, and the God of Isaac, your father. I will give to you and your descendants the land on which you are now lying. Your descendants shall be as many as the dust of the earth and they shall spread out to the west, to the east, to the north, and to the south. Because of you, all the families of the earth shall be blessed. I will protect and watch over you wherever you go. And I will bring you back to this land. This is My promise.''

When Jacob awoke from his sleep, he was frightened. The dream seemed so real! "Surely the Lord is in this place and I did not know it. This is a holy place. It must be the house of God and this must be the gate of heaven!''

In the quiet morning, as the sun spread its warm smile over the earth, Jacob took the stone that had been his pillow and set it upright, a marker for his return. He then poured oil over it and this made the stone holy. He called this place "Beth-El," which means "The House of God." Next, Jacob made a vow, a solemn promise. He said, "If God protects me and brings me back to my father's house safely, then the Lord shall be my God. I will serve Him, and always remember to share with others a part of the good fortune that He has given me.''

When Jacob left this sacred spot, he felt strong and wise. He carried with him the memory of his beautiful dream; and he carried God's promise, forever, deep in his heart.

Jacob and His Two Wives

Jacob left Beth-El, the House of God, and continued his journey back to Haran, the home of his ancestors. From high up on his camel he saw a field with a well in the middle. Three flocks of sheep were lying around, their tongues hanging out of their mouths. Jacob told his camel to kneel down so that he could get off. It is easy to get a camel to lie down; getting him up again is the problem. There were some shepherds also lying around. He asked them, "Where are you from?" When they said they were from Haran, Jacob asked if they knew Laban, his mother's brother.

They replied, "Yes, we know him. He is well. Look, there is his daughter Rachel coming with her sheep."

The sheep all had sad eyes; their heads were drooping and they looked very tired. Jacob said to the shepherds, "It's so hot out here. Since it is not yet time to gather your cattle, why don't you give the sheep water instead?"

The men answered, "We are waiting till all the flocks are here. The stone that covers the well is very heavy. It's a nuisance to roll it away every time some sheep want a drink." They were lazy shepherds.

66

While Jacob was talking, Rachel came near, leading her flock of thirsty sheep. Jacob took one look at Rachel and fell in love. He rolled the heavy stone away from the well all by himself and gave her sheep some water. You can do anything you want to do if you try hard enough. Then he kissed Rachel. Like his father, Isaac, and his mother, Rebekah, he had found his relatives and his future wife all in one day.

Rachel ran home and told her father about Jacob's arrival. Laban came back with her and invited Jacob to stay for a while. Smiling at Rachel, Jacob thought that was a great idea and offered to work with the animals. Jacob got the lazy shepherds to help push his camel upright, and soon the big animal was in Rachel's yard, exchanging grunts and snorts with some new friends.

After a month, Laban said, "Just because you are a relative doesn't mean that you should work for nothing. What shall I pay you?"

Laban had two daughters. The elder daughter, Leah, was a nice, quiet girl. She had long, brown hair, a shy smile, and serious eyes. Rachel was different, with curly hair that went every which way, a mouth that never stopped smiling, and merry eyes. Jacob,

who knew that he had found his true love, told Laban, "I will serve you seven years for Rachel, your younger daughter."

"It is better that I give her to you, my relative, than to another man," said Laban. "You may stay with me."

Jacob worked seven long years for Rachel. Because of his love for her, the days flew by like seconds. When the time was over, Jacob said to Laban, "Please give me my bride, and let us now be married."

So Laban invited all his friends and relatives and gave a big wedding party.

There was singing and dancing and a very good band
Playing all kinds of songs from all over the land.
The guests stayed up late till the stars filled the skies,
Then politely said thank you and waved their good-byes.

In the darkness, as the moon hid its face behind a cloud, Laban brought his daughter to her new husband, Jacob. The girl wore filmy blue and red veils that covered her face and hair. Her perfume was sweet and she spoke in a whisper. Jacob thought his bride was wonderful. But at dawn, as the sun began to chase away the shadows, Jacob had a big surprise: he saw that it was Leah, not Rachel, who had been given to him in the night! Jacob ran out of the house, grabbed Laban, and said, "What have you done to me? Didn't I serve you seven years for Rachel? Why, then, have you deceived me?"

Laban answered, "In our country, it is not the custom to give the younger in marriage before the firstborn. Finish this week of wedding celebrations with Leah and then I will give you Rachel in exchange for seven more years of service."

And so, after a week's time, Jacob took a second bride, his first love, Rachel.

Long ago, it was not unusual for men to have several wives. There were few people then, and this was a good way to increase the population. Leah soon had four sons. Their names were

Reuben, Simeon, Levi, and Judah. Rachel, who was childless, envied Leah and said to Jacob, "Give me children also, or I will die of shame and grief."

Jacob told her, "Only the Lord can decide who shall be born."

"Then take my handmaid," Rachel declared. "She will be a substitute wife for you and I shall adopt her baby." Rachel's handmaid first gave birth to a son named Dan and then had another son named Naphtali.

When Leah saw these two new children, she decided to give her own handmaid to Jacob as another substitute wife. This lady had two sons in a row. Their names were Gad and Asher.

So many wives and so many children,
So many hands to wash, so many feet,
So many wet noses and tears to wipe dry,
And so many birthday presents to buy.

As the years went by, Leah gave birth to two more sons, Issachar and Zebulun. And then God gave her one more child, a beautiful little girl named Dinah.

After all this time, Rachel still had no child of her own. Finally, God blessed her with a son named Joseph. What a wonderful day that was! She thanked God and asked Him to please give her another son. Jacob and his wives now had twelve children, eleven boys and one girl.

One night, Jacob had a dream. God told him, "Leave this land and return to the land of your birth." It was going to be difficult to leave Laban, who would surely miss his daughters and would not like saying good-bye to his grandchildren. And he would certainly miss Jacob. Because of Jacob's hard work, Laban had become a wealthy man. But Jacob always did what the Lord commanded. Besides, he missed his own homeland; it was time to move on.

Jacob put his wives high up on the camels. They sat on cushioned seats under small tents that protected them from sunburn. In their arms they carried the littlest babies. All the other children piled into a cart with big wooden wheels pulled by two strong donkeys. Jacob's cattle followed behind, clanking their bells. Hundreds of curly-haired sheep and long-haired goats trailed along. A short time before, Laban had told Jacob to take all his spotted sheep and all his speckled goats; he had no idea that Jacob would end up with so many. Jacob was a clever man; he knew how to increase his flocks.

Laban was away for three days giving haircuts to his sheep. When he returned, he found out that Jacob had left with his family

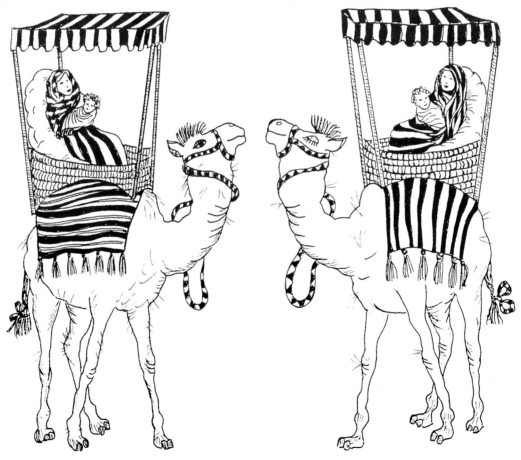

and animals. Laban chased after Jacob all the way to the mountain of Gilead. But one night, God appeared to him in a dream. He said, "Do not do anything bad to Jacob."

Laban listened to God and gave up his angry chase. When Laban did meet up with Jacob, they sat down and talked over their problems. A good talk can cure many bad feelings. Together they built a pillar of stones as a symbol of friendship and then ate a small meal. Laban asked the Lord to watch over Jacob and his family, and they both shook hands, promising never to hurt each other.

In the morning, the grandchildren climbed all over their grandfather Laban. He gave each one a blessing and a big hug and kiss. Leah and Rachel told Laban to be sure to eat right and take care of himself. Jacob named this place "God's Camp." After saying his farewell, Jacob led his big group of people and animals back to Beth-El, the House of God.

Jacob Becomes Israel

The trip back to Jacob's homeland was long and slow. Every so often, the grown-ups had to stop and let the children run around and play games. Baby sheep were always being born and everyone pitched in to help the mothers. The goats, who ate everything in sight, would wander off looking for more food. One of the children would be sent to find them and this took time. The cows had to be milked every day and the camels had to be kept moving, even if it was only in a circle. You know how camels are: lying down is their greatest pleasure. A good deal of time was spent cooking food and washing diapers. There was a lot to do on this trip! But each day, little by little, Jacob's group moved closer to home.

For twenty years Jacob had worried about Esau, his brother. He wondered if Esau was still angry because of the birthright. Now that he was coming home, would Esau want to kill him and his family? Night after night Jacob stayed up, thinking this over. Finally, he had some of his workers take a message to Esau. He said, "Tell Esau that I am coming home from Uncle Laban's country, with many flocks and helpers. And tell Esau that I would like to be his friend." The workers returned and said, "We have seen your brother Esau, and he is coming to meet you with four hundred men." Jacob was really worried now. Remembering how he used to fight with Esau, he imagined the worst: Esau would use these four hundred men to slay Jacob and his people. What was he going to do? He thought about this situation for a long time. All kinds of problems can be solved if you stay calm and think. This is what he decided to do.

First, he divided his big camp into two camps. This way, if one camp was attacked, the other would have a chance to survive. Then, remembering that Esau was fond of possessions, he sent him a big present:

Two hundred she-goats and twenty strong he-goats,
Two hundred lady sheep and twenty big rams,
Thirty camels and colts, forty milk cows, ten bulls,
Twenty fine donkeys and ten little foals.

Jacob thought that Esau might forgive him when he saw all these gifts. He could think of no better way to apologize. As the sun said farewell to the day, Jacob sent his wives and children to a new campground across a small river. Then he spent the night alone. He was waiting for something to happen.

JACOB AND THE STRANGER

Into the dark, a stranger appeared,
He wrestled with Jacob and was to be feared.
For hours on end, till break of light,
Neither one losing or winning the fight.
The stranger said, "Here comes the morning sun,
Let me go now, there is work to be done."
But Jacob held on, though his own thigh was strained,
And said to the man, whose face was now pained,
"Bless me first and then your will shall prevail."
And the stranger said, "You now shall be called 'Israel.'
You have fought the Divine and with men have been strong."
But when Jacob said, "What is your name?" he was gone.

73

Gone like a shooting star, gone like a sigh,
Gone like a dream in the blink of an eye.
Jacob felt blessed, his face shone like the sun,
And from that day to now Jacob's people are one.

As dawn peeked over the rim of the earth, Jacob looked up and saw Esau coming with the four hundred men. He called for his family and helpers to cross back over the little river. They stood in family groups, waiting to greet Esau. Jacob bowed seven times to Esau. He acted as if Esau were a great king and this was the respectful thing to do. The wives and children breathed a sigh of relief as Esau ran to Jacob, threw his arms around him, and gave him a big bear hug and an even bigger kiss! After all this time, Esau had grown up and forgiven Jacob.

It is important to remember that what's past is past. There is always a new day ahead. And one of the best ways to have good tomorrows is to learn to love the person you disliked yesterday.

Jacob stood there, tears of joy falling down his cheeks. Esau was delighted to meet all his new relatives, especially his eleven nephews and Dinah, his niece. At first he politely refused Jacob's gifts, but since he had always liked possessions, it took only a little urging to make him change his mind. He thanked Jacob and said, "Let us continue on the journey. I will lead you." Jacob, who was also being carefully polite, said, "Thank you, but you'd better go on ahead. My group is slow because of all the tiny children and all the animals who are having babies. We will get there as soon as we can." And so Esau went home and waited for his newfound family to arrive.

The long, slow trip continued. It took a while to reach Beth-El, the House of God. In this lovely, green place, God once again spoke to Jacob. He repeated what the stranger who came into the dark had said: "Your name shall no longer be Jacob, but Israel shall be your name." And He told Jacob what He had told his father and grandfather before him: "I am God Almighty. Be fruitful and multiply. Nations shall come from you and also great kings. And I will give to you, and all your descendants, the land that I also gave to Abraham and Issac." Jacob marked this spot with a tall pillar of stone. He poured wine and oil on it to make it holy and named it "The Place Where God Has Spoken."

During this journey, the prayers of Jacob's wife, Rachel, were answered: she gave birth to a second son. But having a baby was difficult during such a hard trip, and Rachel, Jacob's beautiful true love, died. Jacob named his son Benjamin, which means "Child of My Right Hand." And though he missed Rachel, Jacob cried silent tears. This gift of life that she left with him helped give Jacob strength, courage, and great happiness as he slowly brought his people home.

Joseph and His Brothers

Coming home. What a good feeling. After many long years, Jacob was finally coming home! He was excited and ran ahead of his camels, pulling the snorting animals along! But there was sadness waiting. Shortly after he arrived, God called Isaac, Jacob's father, to heaven. Isaac had lived one hundred and eighty years and that was a very long time. With heavy hearts, Jacob and his brother Esau buried their father in the land of Abraham. Although they were sad, they remembered all the happy times they had shared with Isaac, and kept the tears away.

Jacob soon took charge of his father's farm. The boys cared for the speckled sheep and long-haired goats. Jacob's daughter, Dinah, had her own flock of chickens and ducks. Every day she scattered chicken seed and duck food around the barnyard and gathered eggs in a big straw basket. The ladies did the cooking; they scrambled the eggs, made custards and cakes, and baked delicious braided bread for Friday night dinners. Everybody had an important job, even Benjamin, the baby. He did lots of funny things and kept everybody smiling!

Joseph, Jacob's next to last son, was seventeen. His father

would send him out to the fields to help his older brothers feed the sheep and goats. These brothers did not like Joseph, especially when he started telling tales about them. They were terribly jealous of him. They knew that their father loved Joseph more than all his other children because he was the son of Isaac's old age and the child of his first and only true love, Rachel.

It is not wise for parents to have a favorite child. This can create all sorts of troubles. Jacob made this problem worse by giving Joseph a splendid coat of many colors.

It was red and purple and turquoise blue,
Buttercup yellow and green,
A rainbow of colors, fit for a king,
No wonder the brothers felt mean.

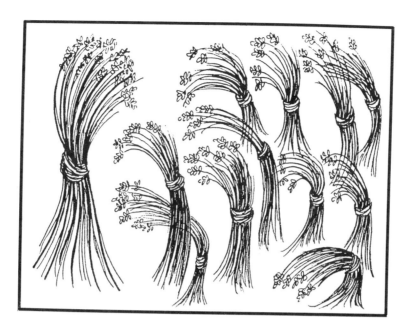

One day, Joseph told his brothers a dream. This turned out to be a big mistake. He said, "We were tying bundles of grain together in the field and your bundles came and bowed down to mine."

His brothers said, "Does this mean that you will rule over us?" They hated him even more for his dreams and his words.

They also felt angry, jealous, and hurt,
They wouldn't include him in games,
They planned dirty tricks,
Wicked, bad, nasty tricks,
And called him all sorts of bad names.

It is sometimes very difficult for older brothers and sisters to admit that a younger child might be more clever than they are. Joseph, not realizing how badly his brothers were feeling, told them another dream. He said, "The sun and the moon and eleven stars bowed down to me."

This time, even Jacob, his father, thought enough was enough and said, "What kind of dream is this? Am I and the whole family going to have to bow down to you?" However, Jacob did keep this dream in his mind. Perhaps his next to youngest son was to become a great ruler someday. He wasn't sure.

One day, Jacob again sent Joseph to the fields. He wanted Joseph to report on how his brothers were doing. From far away, Joseph's brothers saw him coming. He looked like a walking rainbow in his beautiful coat. Before he came near, they made a terrible plan. "Here comes the dreamer," they said. "Let's kill him and throw him in one of these deep pits. We'll tell everyone an evil beast ate him. Then we'll see what will become of his dreams!"

Reuben, the firstborn son, tried to reason with his brothers. "Shed no blood," he said. "Just throw him in the pit but don't hurt him!" Reuben hoped he might be able to rescue Joseph and bring him back safely to his father.

And so, when Joseph came near, his brothers jumped on him, knocked him down, and tore off his coat, his coat of many colors that wrapped around his body like a rainbow. Then they threw him into the empty pit! This was a dreadful deed. Hurting another person never solves problems. And being mean to another, just because you are envious or jealous, is an awful thing to do.

With Joseph trapped in the pit, the brothers sat down and had a nice lunch. During this meal they saw a caravan of Ishmaelites heading toward Egypt. Their camels were loaded with jars of sweet-smelling oils from special trees, boxes of cinnamon, licorice root, cloves and pepper, and medicines for toothaches and headaches. Judah, the fourth eldest brother, began to feel guilty about killing his own flesh and blood. "Let's sell him to the Ishmaelites," he said. "We might as well make some money from this." His brothers thought that was a great idea. While they were congratulating Judah for this new, sneaky plan, a group of traveling salesmen from Midian passed by the pit. Hearing Joseph's cries, they pulled the poor boy up through the narrow opening. And it was these businessmen who sold Joseph, for twenty pieces of silver, to the caravan of Ishmaelites!

Reuben, Jacob's firstborn son, had intended to free Joseph while his other brothers were eating. Returning to the pit, he was shocked to find it empty. "Oh," he cried, "what shall I do?" Because of his birthright, he was responsible for all the younger children. What would he tell his father?

The brothers soon made up another secret plan. They killed a he-goat and dipped Joseph's coat in its blood. Carrying the bloody coat of many colors to their father Jacob, they said, "We found this lying in the dirt. Do you think it belongs to Joseph?"

Jacob answered, "Yes, it is my son's coat. I'm sure that a wild beast has eaten him. My son must have been torn apart into many pieces!" And the old man cried and cried and cried. No one could comfort him. His other sons thought that with Joseph gone they would get more love and attention from their father. How very wrong they were! Jacob wouldn't laugh or tell stories. His mouth turned down at the corners and he walked around by himself, his head full of painful thoughts.

> *His hair turned gray,*
> *He had nothing to say,*
> *His heart was broken in two.*
> *He cried, "Joseph, my child,*
> *Carried off to the wild,*
> *I shall go to my grave mourning you!"*

Joseph in Egypt

Poor Joseph: Thrown into a pit by his brothers, dragged out of the pit by a bunch of traveling salesmen, sold by these salesmen for twenty pieces of silver to the caravan of Ishmaelites, and tied to the hump of a snorting camel all the bumpy way to Egypt! This was just dreadful! Poor Joseph.

When the caravan reached Egypt, the Ishmaelites put the captured boy up for sale. He was bought by Potiphar, the Captain of Pharaoh's guards, who needed someone to work in his big house. Joseph had no choice but to try and make the best of this bad situation. He made good use of his brains and charmed everyone with his sweet personality. Since he never forgot to say his prayers, the Lord stayed with Joseph in this strange land and helped him to do a good job. Joseph worked hard, kept his master's clothes neat, organized the piles of clay tablets and scrolls that were lying around, and kept the cats off the furniture. Potiphar was very pleased. He soon put his new servant-boy in charge of the entire house. The Lord blessed the Egyptian's house for Joseph's sake, and all went well.

Joseph had become a handsome young man. He had curly,

dark hair, big brown eyes with long eyelashes, and a mouth that turned up at the corners. When he walked through the house, all the servant-girls giggled and tried to get his attention. The young ladies in the marketplace followed Joseph with their lowered eyes wherever he went. All the women adored him, especially Potiphar's wife.

"Come and stay with me, Joseph," she would plead.

"No," he said.

"Come and give me just one kiss," she begged.

"No," said Joseph, "I cannot do this great wickedness. It is a sin against God."

"Come and be with me!" she cried, grabbing hold of Joseph's coat.

Not knowing what else to do, Joseph got out of there fast! A little too fast. He left his coat in her hand! Because Joseph had said no to her, Potiphar's wife was determined to get even with him. She took his coat to her husband and told a terrible lie. She said that Joseph tried to kiss her and when she screamed he ran away. And here was his coat to prove it. Poor Joseph. It seemed that coats were always getting him in trouble.

Potiphar became very angry! How could his trusted servant do such a thing! Potiphar believed his wife's story and threw Joseph into prison! This was dreadful! But the Lord stayed with Joseph, gave him strength and courage, and helped him make the best of another bad situation. The Lord caused the keeper of the prison to like Joseph enough to put him in charge of the other prisoners. With the Lord's help, all went well again.

One day, during lunch, Pharaoh found a lightning bug in his cup of wine. "This is disgusting," he said. At dinner that night, a tiny pebble hidden in a sweet cake hurt his tooth. He threw a tantrum and sent both his Cupbearer—the man who poured his wine—and his Number One Baker to the prison. Because they were special prisoners, the captain of the prison guard told Joseph to take good care of them.

One night, the Cupbearer and the Baker both had strange dreams. The next morning, Joseph saw that they were sitting with their heads in their hands. "What's the matter?" he asked. "Why do you both look so sad?"

They replied, "We have had some odd dreams and there is no one here to interpret them."

Joseph said to them, "Since God has sent the dreams, He is the One to interpret them. Tell me your dreams. Maybe God will give me the wisdom to help you."

The Cupbearer told Joseph his dream:

"I saw a vine before me,
Three branches filled with blooms
Which turned, in haste,
To full ripe grapes,
I pressed them into Pharaoh's cup
And gave him juice to taste."

Joseph said to him, "Here is the meaning of your dream. Pharaoh is thinking about the lightning bug in his wine. He is going to decide that it accidently flew into the cup. In three days, Pharaoh will set you free, and you shall once again pour him his cup of wine. But please, when you are released, show kindness to me and remember me. For I was stolen away from the land of the Hebrews, and I have done nothing that should have put me in prison."

The Number One Baker was listening to all this. When he heard the good interpretation of the Cupbearer's dream, he said to Joseph, "I too had a strange dream.

"There were three wicker baskets on my head,
Sweet treats for the King sat on top,
Blackbirds swooped down and pecked at the bread
And I could not make them stop,
No sir,
I could not make them stop."

Joseph told the Number One Baker the sad meaning of his dream. "If you had taken the time to sift your flour carefully, the tiny pebble would not have gotten into Pharaoh's cake. Your carelessness caused Pharaoh to hurt his tooth. Therefore, in your dream, three baskets mean three days. Within three days, Pharaoh shall hang you by your head from a tree, and birds shall eat your flesh.''

Poor Number One Baker. On the third day, both dreams came true, one happy, one sad. But even more sadly, the Cupbearer was so happy to get out of prison that he forgot about remembering Joseph and speaking on his behalf. And so, two more long years went by. Poor Joseph.

One night, Pharaoh woke up shaking in his big golden bed. He had dreamed a very strange dream:

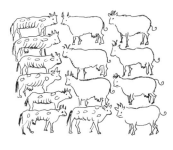

Pharaoh stood by the river, the long river Nile,
Seven fat, lovely cows came to eat for a while,
Then seven more cows, who were ugly and skinny
Came out of the river, the beautiful Nile,
And they ate up the seven, fat, lovely cows.
Pharaoh woke up with a frown
Instead of a smile.

Pharaoh drank a glass of nice, hot goat's milk and fell back to sleep. Another dream wandered through his head:

Seven ears of fine, fat grain
Came up on one strong stalk,
Seven ears of thin grain followed
And swallowed up the fat,
When this scary dream woke Pharaoh up
He said, "Imagine that!"

In the morning, when dreams disappear into the sunlight, Pharaoh was greatly troubled. He called all the wise men of Egypt and asked them to interpret these dreams. Nobody knew what to say. Finally, the Cupbearer spoke. After all this time, he had remembered Joseph! He told Pharaoh about the young Hebrew boy who correctly interpreted his own dream. "Bring him to me!" demanded Pharaoh.

Quickly, the guards fetched Joseph. They gave him a nice haircut, a warm, soapy bath, and dressed him in clean, white clothes. "Does this ever feel good!" thought Joseph. Once again, he looked handsome.

Pharaoh lived in a fancy palace and sat on a golden throne. Beautiful women stood on either side of him, waving fly swatters made of palm branches. This was supposed to help keep Pharaoh cool and bug free. To keep him calm, musicians played the latest flute and harp songs. To keep him amused, acrobats did handstands, jugglers juggled, and magicians pulled rabbits out of hats. Bowls of fruit and nuts were everywhere. When Joseph arrived, Pharaoh was eating a red, ripe pomegranate. He had a special servant who caught the seeds as they were spit out; another servant was the mouth-wiper. Pharaoh finished his snack, licked his lips, and said to Joseph, "I understand that you know the meaning of dreams."

Joseph replied, "It is not me. It is God who will give Pharaoh the meaning and also some good advice."

Pharaoh told Joseph his cow dream and his grain dream. After listening carefully and taking some time to think, Joseph said, "Both dreams are one. God has revealed to Pharaoh what is about to happen:

> *"Seven fat cows mean seven years,*
> *Seven fat ears of grain mean the same,*
> *Seven years of plenty are coming to your land,*
> *More food than you can measure will be at hand,*
> *But seven skinny cows mean seven bad years,*
> *Seven thin ears of grain mean the same,*
> *The good years will be forgotten when the famine comes,*
> *People will go hungry, they will be in pain,*
> *The dream you dreamed was doubled,*
> *Twice you dreamed the same last night,*
> *God has sent these dreams to warn you,*
> *Soon you'll see that God was right."*

Pharaoh was distressed. "Whatever shall I do?" he asked.

Joseph, using all the brain power that God had given him, said, "I think you should find a wise man, someone dependable, and put him in charge of the land. He should be smart enough to appoint good men to gather up part of the grain from the seven good years and put it in giant storehouses. This way, when the seven bad years come, the storehouses can be opened and your people will not starve."

Pharaoh said to Joseph, "Since your God has shown you all this, there must be no man as wise as you. You shall be in charge of my house. My people shall obey your word. You shall be second in command here in Egypt!" Pharaoh gave Joseph a gold ring decorated with his King's sign. He placed a wide gold necklace around Joseph's neck, gave him beautiful, soft, linen clothes, and a new coat of many colors, which wrapped around his body like a rainbow.

And then Pharaoh gave Joseph his very own two-wheeled chariot pulled by a team of white horses, their hair braided in ribbons to match his new coat!

Wherever Joseph went, the people would kneel before him. He went from city to city teaching them how to store their grain. He did the same for those who lived in the country. And after seven good years, a great famine came, just as God had predicted. But thanks to Joseph, the Egyptians were the only people in the world to have food. Joseph opened up the storehouses and there was as much grain as the sand in the sea—probably even more, and much too much to count. The people of Egypt did not starve. They were thankful to Joseph, the wise man, who with God's help understood the meaning of dreams.

Dreams are mysterious things. They come in the night and show pictures inside people's heads. All dreams have meanings, although they are sometimes hard to figure out. God makes dreams to help people understand their lives.

DREAMS

Sometimes dreams are funny,
They make us laugh inside.
Sometimes dreams are scary,
And they make us want to hide.
Some dreams are in color,
Some dreams are black and white,
And they tell stories while we're sleeping
In the middle of the night.

Joseph's Brothers Come to Egypt

In Canaan, life on Jacob's farm had become difficult. Because of the great famine, Joseph's father was having a hard time feeding his big family. When Jacob heard that there was grain in Egypt he told his sons, "Here is some money. Don't lose it. Go down there, and buy us food, so that we may live and not starve."

Ten of the eleven brothers saddled their donkeys, loaded them up with empty sacks, and took off for Egypt. Benjamin, the youngest, stayed at home, out of harm's way.

Joseph, Governor of Egypt, was the man who sold grain to the people. When his brothers arrived, they bowed down to him, their faces touching the earth. Of course Joseph recognized them, but he decided to pretend they were strangers. He spoke roughly to them and asked, "Where are you men from?"

They replied, "From the land of Canaan, to buy food for our starving families."

Joseph remembered the dreams he had told his brothers. And here they were, almost exactly as he dreamed, bowing down in front of him! Because he was a very wise man he thought, "I'm going to test my brothers and see if they have changed their wicked ways."

90

"You are spies," bellowed Joseph, "come to check on my land and its borders!"

"No sir," they said. "We have come only to buy food. We are all one man's sons. Why would he send all of his oldest children to make trouble? That would not make sense."

Joseph roared even louder, "No, you are spies, looking for ways to cross my country's borders in order to invade us!"

The brothers were trembling with fear. Again they replied, "We are the sons of one man from Canaan; the youngest is back with our father and one is gone."

Again Joseph shouted, "You are spies! You shall not return home until your youngest brother comes here! One of you must go home and bring back your brother. This will prove your story. Meanwhile, I'm putting you all in prison to think this over!"

Three days later, Joseph came to the prison and said to his brothers, "Do as I say and live; for I am a God-fearing man.

"If you are as honest as you say,
Then one of you must stay
In prison while the others carry food
To each starving family,
But bring your youngest back to me
As proof, and then
All of you shall live and be free."
This was very hard for Joseph,
He was never mean to men,
But he could not think of another way
To see Benjamin again.

The ten brothers did as they were told. They said to one another, "We are truly so guilty for what we did years ago to our brother Joseph. He pleaded for mercy and we would not help him. That's why this misfortune has come to us."

Reuben said, "Didn't I tell you not to sin against the child? You would not listen and now his blood is being avenged."

The brothers did not know that Joseph, who had been speaking Egyptian to them, understood their language as well. He left the room and wept; he felt badly about how badly his brothers felt. But when he returned he was calm; no one suspected that he had been crying. And he took Simeon from them and tied him up before their eyes! He wasn't through testing his brothers yet.

Joseph ordered his workers to fill the brothers' empty sacks with grain. He also sent along food for the journey back, for themselves and their donkeys. On the road to Canaan, one of the brothers opened his sack to give his donkey some food. There, in the change pocket at the top, was his grain money. "Look," he exclaimed to his brothers, "the money that I paid for the corn has been returned. It is in my change pocket!"

The brothers' hearts stood still. They could not understand such a strange occurrence. "What has God done to us now?" they asked.

When they reached home, they told their father, Jacob, all that had happened: "The Governor of the land of Egypt accused us of being spies. We told him that we had been twelve sons, one is no more, and the youngest lives with our father in Canaan. The Governor said, 'This is how I shall know if you are indeed good men: leave one of your brothers here, go home and take the food to your starving families, and then bring your youngest brother to me. This way I shall know that you are not spies.'"

The brothers took down all their sacks and emptied them in front of Jacob. Each man's money was back in his change purse! This frightened them. Jacob said, "You have taken my children from me. Joseph is no more and Simeon is now gone, tied up in prison. And now you want to take Benjamin away."

Reuben, the eldest, offered, "If anything happens to Benjamin, you may slay my own two sons."

Jacob answered in a loud voice, "Benjamin shall not go down to Egypt with you. His brother is dead and only he is left of my wife Rachel's children. If anything should happen to him, you will have put my gray hairs into the grave!"

The famine was terrible and everybody was getting thin. When the last of the grain had been used, Jacob said to his sons, "Go again to Egypt and buy us a little food."

Judah said to his father, "Remember, the Governor said that we would not see his face unless our youngest brother comes with us. If you will send Benjamin along, we will go down and buy the food."

Jacob asked, "Why have you done such a thing as this to me? Why did you tell the man that you had a brother?"

And they replied, "The man asked us questions about our family. He said, 'Is your father still alive? Do you have another brother?' And we answered him. How could we know that he would say, 'Bring him to Egypt'?"

Judah then spoke. "Send the boy with me, so that all our families may live and not die of hunger. If I don't bring him back, I will bear the blame forever. We are wasting time. We could have been there by now!"

"Very well," said Jacob. "If you are going, take the Governor some nice presents, a little sweet-smelling oil, some dates, honey, cinnamon, cloves, pistachio nuts, and almonds. Take twice the amount of money that you need. Perhaps the money that was returned was a mistake. Give it back. And take your little brother Benjamin. May God have mercy on you and bring you back. If I lose the rest of my children, I lose them. What can I do?"

How sad to be a father
And see your children leaving
For distant lands and dangers.
That's why old Jacob was grieving.

94

I Am Joseph

All the rest of Jacob's sons were now in Egypt: Reuben, Simeon, Levi, Judah, Dan, Naphtali, Gad, Issachar, Zebulun, and young Benjamin. When Joseph saw them he told the head of his house, "Bring all those men inside and make a great feast. They shall dine with me at noon."

The brothers were afraid. Maybe this was a way to capture them and turn them into slaves. Before they walked into Joseph's big house, they told the head servant about the money that had been returned. The head servant said, "I have your money. Your God and the God of your father must have put that treasure in your sacks."

The brothers were becoming more and more confused. Where did the money come from? They were standing around wondering about this when Simeon was brought to them from the prison. The brothers slapped him on the back and hugged him! They were overjoyed to see him again!

Before entering Joseph's house, the brothers washed the sand from their feet and the servants fed the noisy donkeys. Then they waited for Joseph to arrive at noon. As the sundial pointed to twelve, Joseph came in. The brothers gave him the presents and bowed down respectfully. Joseph asked, "How is your father? Is he still alive?"

"He is well," they replied, "and very much alive."

Joseph looked up and saw Benjamin, his mother's youngest son. He said, "And this must be your youngest brother of whom you spoke. God be gracious to you, my son."

After touching Benjamin's cheek, Joseph could not control himself. He ran out of the room, tears pouring from his brown eyes. When he was alone, Joseph cried and cried. After a while he calmed down, washed away the tears, and came back out. "Serve the meal!" he ordered. Two tables were set, one for Joseph, who ate by himself, and one for the brothers. The men were seated according to their ages. This amazed them; they wondered how that had happened.

Reuben was seated at the head,
Simeon by his side.
Levi blessed the glass of wine
As Judah watched with pride.
Dan passed the cup of wine around.
Naphtali took some sips,
And passed it on to Gad who said,
"That's good!" and smacked his lips.
Issachar then took the bread
And raised it in the air.
Zebulun broke off a piece
While Benjamin said this prayer:
"We praise and thank you,
Lord our God,
King of the Universe,
Who gives to us
Bread from the earth."
Then everyone said, "Amen."

Portions from Joseph's table were brought to the other table. They all had a wonderful meal, especially Benjamin; he received five times more food than anyone else!

After the meal, Joseph planned once more to test his brothers' loyalty. He told his head servant, "Fill the men's sacks with as much food as they can possibly carry. Put every man's grain money back in his own change pocket. And put my special silver goblet in the youngest's pocket, along with his money."

As soon as the sun came up, the men and their donkeys were sent home. They thanked Joseph for his hospitality and left, carrying many sacks of food.

When the brothers were not too far away, Joseph told his servant privately, "Follow those men and when you meet up with them say, 'Why have you repaid good with evil? Why have you taken my master's special silver goblet? You have done an evil thing!' "

The servant caught up to the brothers and said what he had been told. The brothers were dumbfounded. "Why do you accuse us?" they asked. "We are honest men. We brought back to you the money that we found in our sacks the first time. Why should we steal silver or gold from your master's house? If anyone here has it, let him die, and we will be your master's slaves."

The servant said, "Only the one who has the special silver goblet shall become a slave. The rest shall be blameless."

The brothers quickly took out their heavy sacks. One by one they opened them for the servant, starting with the eldest and ending with the youngest. The special silver goblet was found in Benjamin's sack! The men could not think straight; they did not know what to do. Loading up their donkeys again, they went back to Joseph's house. Finding Joseph waiting for them, they bowed down in front of him. "What have you done?" demanded Joseph. "Don't you know that a wise man like me will always find out who is a thief?"

Judah said, "What can we say? What words shall we speak? God has discovered that we have been sinful men. All of us shall be your slaves as punishment for the terrible deeds of our past."

But Joseph declared, "I would never do such a thing as that. Only the one in whose sack the goblet was found shall become my slave. As for the rest of you, go home in peace to your father."

Judah came near to Joseph and said in a quiet voice, "Oh my lord, let me speak a word in your ear:

"*A little while ago you asked us if we had a father,*
Or a perhaps a little brother left at home.
We said unto my lord, we have an old man for a father
And a child of tender years, and he alone
Is left of Rachel, lovely Rachel,
His beautiful own mother
Who is living now in heaven
With Joseph, his true brother.
His father, Jacob, loves him dearly,
And though he let us bring him here
So that you could see him clearly,
He is living in great fear.

You see, his wife bore him two fine young sons
And one of them's been taken,
Torn to pieces by some wild beasts
And our father remains shaken.
'If you take this little one,' he said,
'And if harm comes his way,
I shall bring my gray hairs down
Into the grave with me today.'
His soul is bound up with this child,
And with his other being dead
I cannot bear to see him mourn again.
I beg you please, take me instead!"

Hearing the sadness that had overtaken his father, Joseph cried out to the servants around him, "All of you! Leave!" When they were gone, Joseph made himself known to his brothers. Tears once again appeared in his eyes as he said, "I am Joseph. Is it really true that my father, Jacob, is still alive?"

His brothers stood with their mouths open. They really couldn't believe this! "Come near," said Joseph. "I am Joseph, your brother, whom you sold into Egypt. Do not be upset or angry with yourselves because of what you did. There is a reason for everything in this world. God has sent me here to preserve life. The great famine has lasted two years so far; five more bad years are to come. God put me here to make sure that your children and all your descendants shall live according to the blessing of Abraham. He helped me become a good friend to Pharaoh and a ruler over Egypt. Now hurry. Go to our father and give him this message from me: 'God has made your son Joseph lord over Egypt. Come down here fast. You shall dwell in the good green pastures of Goshen. And you shall be near to me, you and your children, and your children's children, and all your flocks and herds. I promise to take care of you. Remember, there are five more bad years to come.' "

Then Joseph, the great Governor of Egypt, put his head down on Benjamin's neck and wept tears of joy. Joseph kissed all of his brothers and they started crying. Everyone in Joseph's house heard them and soon found out what was going on. Good news travels almost as fast as bad news.

When Pharaoh learned that Joseph's brothers had come, he was very pleased. He loved Joseph and was happy for him. Pharaoh ordered wagons with big wooden wheels sent to Canaan to pick up Jacob and all the wives and children. He said, "Bring your father. Tell him to leave his old stuff behind. All the wonderful goods of Egypt will be his!"

Joseph did what Pharaoh ordered and gave his brothers wagons and food and new clothes. His youngest brother, Benjamin, received three hundred pieces of silver and five changes of clothing! Joseph couldn't do enough for him! To Jacob, he sent ten he-donkeys, loaded down with all the good things of Egypt, and ten she-donkeys, carrying all kinds of food. As his brothers were leaving, Joseph told them, "Behave yourselves. I don't want to hear about any fighting or arguments on your trip!"

Jacob was helping his daughter, Dinah, feed the chickens and ducks when he saw the long line of men, wagons, and noisy donkeys coming toward the farm. "What in the world is all this?" he thought.

"Father, Father," called his sons. "Joseph is alive and he is ruler over Egypt!"

Jacob's heart was pounding! He could not believe them! He was speechless! After listening to the words Joseph had told them to say, he looked at the wagons sent by his son, and he once again felt happy. "I believe you," he said when he could finally speak. "My son Joseph is alive. I will go and see him before I die."

That night, God came to Jacob in a dream. "Jacob, Jacob," He said.

"I am here," answered Jacob.

The Lord said, "I am God, the God of your father; do not fear going to Egypt. I will make you into a great nation there. I will go with you to Egypt and I will also surely bring you back home again."

Jacob's sons put their father, their wives, and all the children into the wagons sent by Joseph. The noisy donkeys did all the pulling. Speckled sheep and long-haired goats followed along behind. Dinah's chickens and ducks and one fat goose wandered all over the place; it was hard keeping them together. The milk cow swished her tail and clanked her cow bell, and Jacob's old, snorting

camels carried the eleven brothers high up on their humps. From the back of his wagon, Jacob looked around at the farm, put good memories into his head, and left Canaan.

The family made its way to Goshen, the nicest part of Egypt. They were met there by Joseph in his beautiful two-wheeled chariot. When Joseph saw his father, Jacob, he put his arms around him and cried and cried and cried. Crying is something that everybody has to do once in a while. Tears wash away the bad times and help shine up your face for better days ahead. Jacob said to Joseph, "Now I can die, because I have seen your face."

Joseph brought his father to the palace and introduced him to Pharaoh. "How old are you?" asked Pharaoh.

"I am one hundred and thirty years, although my father and my grandfather lived longer," replied Jacob.

Jacob then asked God's blessing for Pharaoh, the king who had been so kind to his beloved son, Joseph. And he blessed all his sons and said, "May they become a great people and be called forevermore by my name, the Children of Israel."

Exodus

שמות

Child of the Nile

The children of Israel had many children,
And these fine Hebrew children had many more,
They prayed to the Lord and were mighty and strong,
The whole land of Egypt was filled with their song.
But a new king was crowned, who did not remember
How Joseph had saved the Egyptians from dying.
"These people are mighty," he said. "They may fight us
By helping our enemies try to destroy us.
I shall make them my slaves,
Soon the strong will be crying for mercy from Pharaoh,
The greatest of kings."
The Children of Israel, despite all these cruel things,
Grew mightier yet, till Pharaoh decreed,
"The midwives must kill all the boy children born
To the Hebrews. In this way their power will cease."
But the midwives feared God and the babies survived.
Pharaoh spoke with them harshly, his anger revived.
He said, "Israel's, Children will no longer smile.
All their newly born sons must be thrown in the river,
The beautiful river, the long river Nile.

105

I'll get rid of these Hebrews one way or another!"
The king did not know that a wise Hebrew mother
Would think of a way to save her sweet child,
All cheerful and chubby, with rosy, red cheeks
And a dimple that showed up whenever he smiled.
He was good, he was quiet,
And nobody heard him for three months
Until he was too big to hide.
Then his wise Hebrew mother made him a boat.
It was woven of tall weeds that grew alongside
The beautiful river, the long river Nile.
And on top of a soft feather pillow inside,
She placed the sweet child and then told his sister,
"Pharaoh's own daughter will bathe here today.
Watch and see if she finds him as he floats away."
When Pharaoh's own daughter came down to the water,
She heard what she thought was a baby's soft cry.
She told one of her handmaids to fetch from the river
The small woven boat as it floated on by.
She lifted the lid and to her surprise
Saw a curly-haired baby with tears in his eyes.
Pharaoh's own daughter, gentle and kind, said,
"This must be a Hebrew, this child I have found."
His sister, appearing without any sound, said,
"Shall I call a nurse to take care of this baby?"
The woman said, "Go! Find one for me please!"
The girl brought her mother and when the child saw her
He started to laugh and kick up his feet.
"I'd love to care of a baby this sweet,"
Said the child's happy mother. "It would be a nice treat."
"I'll pay you good wages to nurse him for me.
And when he is ready, my son he shall be,"
Said Pharaoh's own daughter.
"And his name shall be Moses, Child of the Nile,
This sweet little child drawn out of the water.
This wonderful baby has made us all smile!"

Moses Grows Up

Moses was a lucky child. He had two mothers loving him: Jochebed, who gave him life, and Pharaoh's daughter, who rescued him from death. These good women would always try to do what was best for their sweet child.

When he was a baby, Moses lived with his mother, Jochebed, his father, Amran, and his sister and brother, Miriam and Aaron. As she rocked Moses to sleep, Jochebed sang Hebrew lullabies. When he was awake, she would repeat over and over the special prayers of his people, the Children of Israel. As Moses grew older, Jochebed told him stories about his famous ancestors, Abraham, Isaac, and Jacob. He loved the story about Noah's Ark, he couldn't wait to hear what happened to Isaac on the mountain, and he could recite all the names of Joseph's brothers by heart.

Every day, Jochebed taught Moses something new. The most important lesson that he learned was about God and His promise to someday return the Israelites to their land. "God did not create people to become slaves," said Jochebed. Moses listened carefully; he would remember everything that his mother said, forever.

When he was a young boy, Jochebed brought Moses to the palace to meet his new mother, Pharaoh's daughter. "Remember your manners, my son," said Jochebed. "Always say 'please and thank you,' wipe your mouth after you eat, and be sure to say 'excuse me' if you bump into anyone. Fold your clothes and don't lose your sandals. Brush your teeth, wash your hands, and wipe the sand from your feet before you get into bed. And one more thing: Always remember that you are a Hebrew. Do not forget your God!" She kissed Moses and told him that she would see him from time to time. Then, as tears began to fill her eyes, Jochebed, the true mother of Moses, said good-bye.

Pharaoh's daughter was overjoyed to finally have her adopted son living with her. She was delighted to see how handsome he had become and was pleased that he behaved so nicely. Moses was given a lovely room and beautiful new clothes. He had a special schoolroom where he learned to write on clay tablets and do math problems in the sand. Because he was a good student, Pharaoh's daughter gave him a wonderful present: his own shiny black horse. As the years went by, Moses learned to be a leader of men. He was honest and fair and, most of all, he was kind. But during his time at the palace, Moses always remembered what his mother had taught him: he was born a Hebrew and was never to forget his God.

One day, when Moses was all grown up, he went out to visit the brickyards. This was where the Hebrew slaves worked under terrible conditions. He was filled with pity as he watched his people bent over in pain and exhaustion. Moses was very upset when he saw a Hebrew slave being whipped by a cruel, Egyptian master. After all, these were his people. He looked this way and that, and when he saw that no one was watching, he killed the cruel Egyptian and hid him under a pile of sand.

The next day, he again went out to the brickyards. This time, he saw two Hebrews fighting with each other. "Why are you hitting your fellowman?" he asked one of them.

The man said, "Who made you a prince and a judge over us? Are you thinking of killing me like you killed the Egyptian?"

Moses turned cold with fear! "If these two men know what I did, then surely Pharaoh will find out and come after me!" he thought. "I'd better leave Egypt at once!"

Moses walked for miles and miles across the hot desert. Wind storms knocked him down and sand storms stung his face. Thirsty and sunburned he moved slowly over this great, empty space under the ever-changing desert sky.

THE DESERT SKY

Red is the color of the desert sky
At dawn when the day is new.
Yellow is the color of the desert sky
When the sun comes into view.
White is the color of the desert sky.
White is the color of the sand
When noontime comes and the white heat
Spreads like paint across the land.
Pink is the color of the desert sky,
Soft like the evening breeze.
Purple is the color of the desert sky
When the sun bids a sad good-bye.
Black is the color of the desert sky
Till the moon and the stars appear.
Then silver and gold fill the desert sky
And the wonders of God are near.

Moses walked on and on until he reached the land of Midian. One night, as he lay by a well, he looked up and saw seven beautiful women coming to get water for their flocks. These were the daughters of the priest of Midian, a very important person. They filled the big water basin and were about to give their sheep a drink when some impolite shepherds pushed them out of the way and led their own sheep to the water. Moses, who always tried to help people in trouble, got up and chased away these bullies. He then helped the beautiful maidens give water to their sheep. The maidens said thank you and went back to their big tent.

Their father said, "Why have you returned so soon today?"

They explained that a kind Egyptian chased away the bad shepherds and helped them to water their flocks.

"Where is he?" asked their father. "Bring him here to eat bread with us!"

Moses was happy to come to the tent of Jethro, the priest of Midian. The seven beautiful daughters brought him platters of food and goblets of wine and then they danced for him. What a lovely treat that was! They wore rainbow-colored dresses, vests made of jangling silver coins, blue and purple veils, and as they twirled around, their long, dark hair floated behind them. Moses relaxed on a nice, plump cushion; for just a moment he was able to forget the sadness that had forced him to walk across the desert, away from Pharaoh's anger.

Jethro asked Moses if he would like to have his daughter Zipporah for a wife. This made Moses very happy. They were married, and soon they had a baby boy to love. Moses named him Gershom, which means, "I Was a Stranger in a Strange Land." Moses had not forgotten his people.

God Speaks to Moses

During the long time that Moses lived in Midian, Pharaoh, the king of Egypt, died. The new king was very mean and the Hebrew slaves were suffering greatly. God heard their sad cries and decided to help them leave Egypt and go to the land of Abraham, Isaac, and Jacob. And He had found the perfect leader for them, a good man to trust with such a difficult job.

Moses was a kind and thoughtful shepherd. He would lead his flocks carefully through the thorny bushes, and he often carried lost sheep back to their mothers. He was an intelligent man who enjoyed asking questions, and he was curious about everything that went on around him. One day, as he tended his flock in the wild country near Mount Horeb, he noticed, out of the corner of his eye, an amazing sight: a small thorn bush was burning with fire and it was not destroyed! Moses said, "I must turn around and see this great miracle. I can't imagine why that bush has not burned up."

From the midst of the burning bush, the Lord God called, "Moses, Moses."

"I am here," answered Moses, dumbfounded at the thought of a talking burning bush.

And God said, "Take off your shoes. The place where you are standing is holy ground. I am the God of your father, of Abraham, Isaac, and Jacob." Moses hid his face from such wonder; he was afraid to look at God.

The Lord said, "I have seen the sorrows of My people who are slaves in Egypt. I have heard their sad cries. I have come to deliver them out of the hands of the cruel Egyptians. Come now, I will

send you to Pharaoh. You will bring My people, the Children of Israel, out of Egypt."

Moses said to God, "I am only a shepherd. How can I go to Pharaoh and do such a big job?"

"I will be with you and help you all the way," replied the Lord. "And when you return, you shall pray to Me right here, upon this very mountaintop called Mount Sinai."

Moses had some more questions for God. He asked, "When I tell the people that the God of their fathers has sent me, they will say, 'What is His name?' What shall I tell them?"

God said, "Tell them 'I Am That I Am.' This means: Do not fear. I will be with them and save them. They must keep their faith in Me. Gather the elders of Israel together and tell them that I will bring them up from Egypt to a wonderful land flowing with milk and honey. Then go to the king of Egypt and say, 'The Lord, God of the Hebrews, has met with us. Allow us to go for three days in the desert so that we may worship and make a sacrifice to Him.' Now I know that he won't let you go unless something really dramatic happens. This is what I intend to do: I will stretch out My hands and Egypt will be knocked down by My words. After that, he will let you go. I will make sure that the Egyptian people are friendly to you and help you to leave easily. Tell every woman to ask her neighbors and friends for a gift of silver or gold jewelry and some pretty clothing for the children. This way they will leave with some nice remembrances of the good people of Egypt and not just with bad thoughts of the evil Pharaoh."

Moses kept thinking up more problems. He said, "Perhaps the people will still not believe me. They will say, 'How do we know that the Lord has appeared to you?' "

The Lord said, "What is that in your hand?"

"A shepherd's rod," answered Moses.

"Throw it on the ground!" commanded God.

Moses did as he was told and the rod became a serpent! Moses jumped back; he wasn't too fond of snakes. "Take it by the tail!" ordered God. The snake became a rod again!

"I will teach you to perform other marvelous signs," said God to Moses.

Once more, Moses tried to tell God that he felt unworthy of such an important task. He said, "Oh Lord, I am not a man of many words. I do not speak well; my tongue is slow."

The Lord said to him, "Who has given man a mouth? Who has made him speechless, or hard of hearing, with good eyes or blind, if not I, the Lord? Now go. I will be with your mouth and teach you what to say!"

"Oh Lord," cried Moses, "send anyone but me!"

The Lord was patient with Moses. "Your brother Aaron is coming to see you," He said. "I know that he can speak well. Here is my final plan: I shall tell you what to say and you shall put the words in his mouth. He shall speak for Me through you. Take this magic rod, perform the signs that I have taught you, and bring our people home!"

Before he could begin his journey, Moses thought it would be polite to ask permission from his father-in-law, Jethro, who had been so kind to him in Midian. "Go in peace," said Jethro. And so Moses placed his wife Zipporah, and his two sons, Gershom and Eliezer, on donkeys, and they all began the long journey to Egypt.

During the trip, Moses met his brother Aaron on the Mountain of God. They were so happy to see each other; it had been such a long time! After they kissed and hugged, Moses repeated all the words of the Lord to Aaron and showed him the magic signs that he would be using. They continued the trip back to Egypt and immediately gathered together all the elders of the Children of Israel. Aaron spoke the words of God, and when the people saw the magic signs, they were convinced that they were about to be saved. And when they heard that the Lord had remembered the Children of Israel and had seen their suffering, they thanked God by bowing their heads and saying grateful prayers:

We thank the Lord for His kindness,
For His mercy everlasting.
We thank the Lord, the God of gods.
Praises to Him we bring.
We thank the Lord for His wonders,
For His mercy everlasting,
For the sun, the moon, the stars at night.
Praises to Him we bring.
We thank the Lord for His goodness,
For His mercy everlasting,
For remembering us in our time of pain.
Praises to Him we bring.

Let My People Go

After seeing the magic signs and hearing the words of God, the Children of Israel had great confidence in Moses and Aaron. The two brothers soon came before Pharaoh and spoke these words: "The Lord, the God of Israel, has said, 'Let My people go, so that they might hold a celebration for Me in the wilderness.' "

Pharaoh asked, "Who is this Lord, that I should listen to His voice and let Israel go? I don't know this Lord and I will not let Israel go!" Pharaoh had never heard of God; he was busy worshiping his Egyptian idols and sacred animals.

Moses and Aaron explained, "The God of the Hebrews has met with us. Please let us go for three days into the wilderness so that we may offer a sacrifice to the Lord our God. If we don't, He may strike us down with sickness or death."

Pharaoh shouted, "Moses and Aaron, why do you interrupt the people's work with this talk? It's only an excuse for a vacation. Get back to work!"

That same day, Pharaoh made life even more difficult for the Children of Israel. He told the Hebrew work officers, "You shall no longer give your people straw to make the bricks hold together.

They will have to go out and gather their own straw. But they must make the same amount of bricks as before. They have nothing better to do; that's why they are whining!''

The work officers gave the people their new orders and they scattered all over Egypt looking for straw. "Fulfill your job the same as before when you had straw," they ordered.

> *The poor Hebrew slaves were moaning;*
> *This order would not be filled.*
> *They could find no straw to make the bricks.*
> *Surely they'd all be killed!*

When Pharaoh's guards saw that the Hebrew work officers had been unable to get the slaves to fill their daily quota of bricks, they gave the officers a beating. These officers came and complained to Pharaoh, "Why do you deal with your servants this way? You ask us to make bricks, yet there is no straw given to us. Because of this we are beaten. This work is impossible to do!"

Pharaoh screamed, "You are lazy, you are lazy! That's why you say, 'Let us go so we may sacrifice to the Lord.' Get back to work!"

When they left Pharaoh, the work officers met Moses and Aaron, who were waiting outside. Angrily they said, "The Lord will punish you because you have made us hateful in the eyes of Pharaoh and his men. You have helped put a sword into their hands to kill us!"

Moses felt awful. He needed someone to talk to, a good friend. A good friend is always there for you, always willing to listen and help out with problems. God was Moses' best friend. Moses could talk to Him and, since he trusted God, he paid close attention to everything He said. Moses asked God, "Lord, why have You dealt so badly with these people, and why in the world did You send me? Ever since I came to speak to Pharaoh in Your name and rescue Your people, he has behaved worse than before. You have not delivered Your people at all!"

"Now you shall see what I will do to Pharaoh," said the Lord. "The power of God will force him to let the Children of Israel go!"

And God spoke to Moses saying, "I am the Lord; I have heard the moaning of the Children of Israel. I have remembered my promise to Abraham, Isaac, and Jacob. Tell the people this: I will deliver you from bondage with an outstretched arm. There will be great punishments coming to the cruel Egyptians. You will be My people and I will be your God. You will know that I am the Lord your God, who brought you out from slavery. I will bring you to the Promised Land. I am the Lord!"

Moses told the Children of Israel what God had said, but they would not listen. They were disappointed; they had been slaves for such a long time.

Again the Lord spoke to Moses and said, "Go in, speak to Pharaoh, and tell him to let the Children of Israel go out of his land."

Moses said, "But if the Children of Israel haven't listened to me so far, how then can I expect Pharaoh to listen to me? My speech is so very slow."

The Lord said to Moses, "I told you before that I would tell you what to say and Aaron would speak for Me through you. He will tell Pharaoh to let the Children of Israel leave. However, I will

make Pharaoh stubborn; he will not let you go. But don't worry. I will increase my signs and wonders in Pharaoh's country. I will use My power over Egypt and bring My people, the Children of Israel, out of slavery. The Egyptians will know that I am the Lord."

Moses and Aaron felt much better. The spirit of God was with them and they did as the Lord commanded.

Moses was eighty years old and Aaron was eighty-three when they went to speak to Pharaoh. They were very brave men. The Lord gave Moses these instructions: "When Pharaoh says to you, 'Show us a sign to prove that your God is so mighty,' tell Aaron to take your rod and throw it down on the ground. It will become a serpent before Pharaoh's eyes."

Moses and Aaron went in to Pharaoh and did as the Lord commanded. The rod became a wiggling, slippery serpent! Pharaoh called all the wise men and magicians of Egypt, and they managed to do the same magic trick with their rods. Snakes were slithering all over the place. But Aaron's magic snake-rod opened up a gigantic mouth and swallowed up all the other magic snake-rods! Still, Pharaoh's heart was hardened. He was stubborn, just as God had predicted. He would not listen and he would not let the Israelites go!

The Lord then gave Moses more instructions: "Here is My first big plan. In the morning, go down to the water where Pharaoh prays to his river gods. Carry your rod with you. Tell Pharaoh this: The Lord, the God of the Hebrews, sent me to tell you to let My people go so they may worship Me in the wilderness. But since you have not listened, you will soon know that I am the Lord. When this rod touches the river, all the water in Egypt will turn to blood. The fish will die, the river will smell, and no one will be able to drink!"

This was the first of ten terrible plagues that the Lord had waiting for Pharaoh.

The Ten Plagues

Blood, blood, and the rivers turned red.
Aaron did what Moses said.
He took the rod, stretched out his hand,
And blood flowed swiftly through the land.
Ponds and pools began to stink.
There was no more water fit to drink.
Seven days passed, then Aaron said to Pharaoh,
"The Lord has commanded, 'Let My people go!'
If you refuse to do the Lord's bidding,
He will fill your land with frogs
And He's not kidding!
Frogs, frogs, all over the place,
You'll find them in your bed,
They'll be jumping on your face!"
Aaron took the rod, stretched out his hand,
And little green frogs covered all the land.
They leaped into the ovens.
They got into the bread.
The dough was hopping all around till Pharaoh said,

"Tell the Lord to take these frogs away from me,
If he does that, then I'll set your people free."
Moses asked the Lord for help
And He said, "Tomorrow I'll deliver
All the frogs away from here except the ones in the river."
When Pharaoh saw at last that there was some relief,
He hardened his heart and gave the Hebrews more grief.
So the Lord said to Moses,
"Tell Aaron, if you please,
To touch your rod upon the earth
And I'll turn the dust to fleas."
Fleas, fleas were everywhere,
Their little eggs kept hatching.
Cats and dogs and cows
And even cockroaches were scratching.
But the king's heart was hardened.
He wouldn't hear the Hebrews' cries.
God told Moses, "Have Aaron say,
'Look out Pharaoh, here come flies!
Flies, flies, swarms of flies,
Their bites will make your people swell.
But they'll be no flies in Goshen
Where the Hebrew children dwell.
By tomorrow you will see your people swatting day and night.' "
And when Pharaoh saw the swarms of flies he said,
"You're right! You're right!
I'll let you go to serve your Lord
If He'll make these pests depart."
The Lord did as Moses asked Him,
But Pharaoh hardened up his heart.
Then the Lord told Moses to tell Pharaoh,
"If you still refuse
To let My people go, then I have very nasty news.
The Lord's hand is on your cattle grazing on the plain.
These herds and all your other flocks will soon be slain.
But the cattle of My children, the Israelites, shall live."

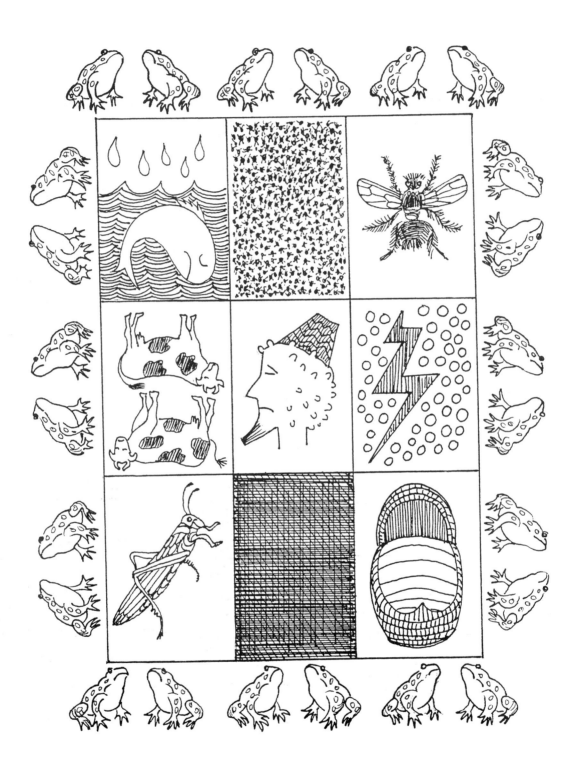

The next day Egypt's cattle died, but Pharaoh wouldn't give
An inch.
He wouldn't budge,
He wouldn't let the people go,
So God told Moses to tell Aaron,
"Take some soot from down below
And throw it toward the sky,
Right in front of Pharaoh."
Now this seemed rather simple,
Except the soot turned into dust
That gave Egyptians big red pimples.
But just as God had said,
Pharaoh still would not agree
To let the Hebrew Children of Israel go free.
The Lord told Moses to tell Pharaoh,
"I shall cause a storm of wonder."
And when Aaron stretched the rod up, there was hail
And there was thunder.
Every tree was broken, lightning flashed, the crops were taken,
But in the land of Goshen, the Israelites were not forsaken.
Pharaoh said to Moses and to Aaron,
"I have sinned. Please tell your God
To stop the hail and stop the thunder,
And please put down your magic rod!"
And Moses prayed and very soon the thunder and hail ceased,
But Pharaoh lied and would not let the Hebrews be released.
Aaron said to Pharaoh, "If you do not let us leave,
The Lord God of the Hebrews has a worse plague up His sleeve.
Locusts, locusts eating every plant and every tree!"
But Pharaoh said, "Only your men may go,
Now get away from me!"
When it was morning Pharaoh looked and saw a big, black cloud
Moving quickly toward his farmland.
They ate everything in sight.
Pharaoh called for Moses and for Aaron
And said, "All right! All right!

I have sinned against the Lord your God.
If he helps, I'll let you go!"
When God heard Pharaoh's wishes,
He caused a strong west wind to blow.
And the locusts disappeared,
There were no bugs left on his borders,
But Pharaoh's heart was hardened
And he canceled his new orders.
The Lord now said to Moses, "Toward heaven stretch your hand.
A terrifying darkness shall fall upon this land."
Dark, dark, the world was dark,
Day turned into night,
Except in Goshen, where God's children lived
Surrounded by His light.
Pharaoh said, "You may go now, but leave your flocks behind."
Moses and Aaron told him, "No. You are not being kind!
We need our flocks to serve our God
In thanks for His reward."

Pharaoh wouldn't let them go;
His heart was hardened by the Lord.
Then in great anger Pharaoh yelled,
"Get away from me! Good-bye!
The day you see my face again,
That very day you'll die!"
Aaron said, "You've spoken well,
We'll see your face no more!"
Then the Lord God said to Moses,
"There is one more plague in store.

I'm sure that he will throw you out
As soon as it is done.
Please speak to all your people.
Tell them to ask everyone,
Their good neighbors,
Their new friends and old,
To give them gifts of friendship,
Jewels of silver and of gold."

Then Moses said and Aaron spoke these words in Pharaoh's ear,
"At midnight God will go out into Egypt without fear.
All the firstborn of this land shall die.
Beware. The time is near.
And there shall be a great cry heard all over Egypt land,
But Israel's Children shall be safe beneath God's hand."
Moses and Aaron left the king, their anger showing through.
"Remember," said God, "his heart is hard.
Now here's what you're to do:
Let every family take a year-old lamb for all to eat.
Then take its blood and smear it on their houses in the street.
The two side posts shall have this mark
And the beam above their head.
Then they should eat the roasted meat
With bitter herbs and unleavened bread.
They must keep their shoes on in the house
And be ready to leave fast.
Tell them to eat as quickly as they can

For it soon will come to pass
That I will kill the firstborn, man and beast,
Throughout the land of Egypt,
But when I see the blood upon your houses I'll protect
And pass over you.
And you shall keep this day forevermore,
A memorial to Me Who kept destruction from your door."
God's words were told to Aaron
And he in turn told Israel's children
To do as God commanded, to stay inside and keep well hidden.
And it came to pass at midnight,
The Lord God did as He had said.
All of Egypt's firstborn,
Including Pharaoh's son, were dead.
And there rose up a cry in Egypt.
Not one house remained untouched.
Pharaoh called for Moses and for Aaron. He said,
"This is too much!
Rise up and leave my land. Take all your flocks and go away!"
And this great night, this great Passover,
Reminds us to this day
How God brought His Hebrew children out from under Pharaoh's hand,
And led them on their journey back
Into the Promised Land.

The Exodus

As the morning star greeted the sun, the Children of Israel said farewell to Egypt. From north, south, east, and west, thousands and thousands of men, women, and children streamed out of their houses and became part of the biggest caravan ever. On their backs, wrapped in cloaks, they carried mixing bowls full of unleavened bread.

Bread takes a long time to make. First you mix the dough, knead it with your hands, let it rise, punch it down, knead it some more, and let it rise again. The Children of Israel had to leave quickly; they had no time to wait for the dough to rise. Someday, when they were finally in the Promised Land, they would once again bake wonderful challahs, raisin breads, and poppyseed bagels.

LEAVING

The Children of Israel carried their lives
Upon their backs, and on top of carts
Pulled by donkeys and cows.
The children and wives

129

Sat on top of blankets and held onto jewels
Of silver and gold
That their neighbors in Egypt
Gave them as gifts
To remember them by.
The caravan moved
As the sun in the sky
Journeyed slowly through daytime
And into the night.
There were huge flocks of sheep,
Flocks of ducks and of chickens,
And hungry old goats eating
Everything in sight.
Donkeys were braying
And horses were neighing,
Camels were snorting and
What a surprise!
They didn't need pushing to get them to hurry!
They were happy to rise,
And scurried away
With big loads of pots, pans, and people.
On that glorious day,
Their humps soon were swaying
In time with the songs that the Israelites sang
As they marched out of Egypt,
To a place, green and sunny,
To freedom in God's land
Of sweet milk and honey.

When Pharaoh let the Israelites go, God did not take them on the shortcut through the land of the Philistines. The Philistine people were rough and tough and always fighting. God did not want the Children of Israel to see the results of war and become afraid. So He took them the long way around, through the wilderness by the Sea of Reeds. Moses gently carried the bones of Joseph with him. Long ago, Joseph asked the Israelites to make him a promise. He said, "God will surely remember you; when that happens, please be sure to carry my bones away from here with you."

The Lord did not want His people to get lost. During the day, He formed Himself into a gigantic gray pillar of cloud to lead the way. At night, He became a long red pillar of fire that brightened the dark. In this way He made sure that the great caravan would be able to travel in the right direction both day and night.

When the king of Egypt heard that the Children of Israel had fled, he had a change of heart. In his great hurry to let them go after the last terrible plague, he didn't realize that he was losing all his slaves. "What is this we have done!" he cried.

Pharaoh sent for his golden chariot, pulled by two strong, black horses, and called up his mighty army. There were six hundred heavy-duty chariots pulled by teams of white, black, and brown horses with fancy red plumes on their heads. Smaller chariots followed behind, the horses' reins wrapped around the riders' waists. This kept their hands free to shoot the big bows and arrows. Pharaoh's top officers were cracking their whips and shouting, making the shiny horses run faster and faster, their hooves thundering as they raced toward the Israelites. The strongest warriors in Egypt marched behind, carrying long, sharp spears. What a fearsome sight they were!

As night fell, the Children of Israel set up camp on the shores of the Sea of Reeds. They were tired and needed to rest. Suddenly they heard chariot wheels screeching, hundreds of hooves pounding, and men's voices roaring across the wilderness! Looking up, they saw the Egyptians coming after them! This frightened them greatly! The Israelites cried out to the Lord and said to Moses, "Is it because there are no graves in Egypt that you brought us away to die here in the wilderness? We would have been better staying slaves in Egypt!" The people were about to give up hope; they were losing their faith.

Moses said to them, "Have no fear. Stand by and see how the

Lord will save you today. As surely as you now see the Egyptians, you shall never see them again. The Lord will win this battle for you. Wait! Keep your peace!"

Freedom is not easily won. You must work hard for it, just like you work hard to get a good grade or to win a race. Though it may look like you won't succeed, if you keep your faith, all things are possible. Moses trusted the Lord and kept his faith. He knew God would not let His people down.

Then the Lord said to Moses, "Don't come crying to Me. Speak to the Children of Israel! Go forward and act! Lift up your rod, stretch out your hand over the sea, and divide it. The Children of Israel shall walk into the sea on dry ground. I will harden the hearts of the Egyptians and they will follow after them. Then watch and see: the Egyptians will soon know that I am the Lord!"

The pillar of cloud that had been in front of the people now came between the Egyptians and the Israelites. God's magic cloud and the darkness of night prevented the Egyptians from seeing what was happening. Then, as Moses stretched his hand out over the sea, the Lord caused a strong east wind to blow all through the night. The sea separated in two directions, as if someone were pulling it back like a big curtain. The Children of Israel went into the sea on dry ground, the waters forming a wall on either side of them, like fountains flowing backward.

Egyptians pursuing,
Into the sea!
All Pharaoh's horses,
Into the sea!
Chariots and riders,
Into the sea!
Beneath fire and cloud
The thundering crowd
Of Egyptians were
Panicked!
They fell
With a thud,

132

Wheels locked
In the mud!
Chariots falling,
Into the sea!
They cried,
"Let us flee!
Israel's Lord
Is fighting
Against us and
Won't let us be!
He's thrown
Pharaoh's army
Into the sea!"

Then the Lord said to Moses, "Stretch out your arm over the sea, so that the waters may come back upon the Egyptians, and upon their chariots and riders."

Moses held out his arm over the sea and as the sun awakened the new day, the sea began to flow forward again. The Egyptians were so confused that they ran toward the huge waves! In this way, the Lord caused the Egyptians to be hurled into the sea, the waters covering all the chariots and riders. Pharaoh's entire army drowned! But the Children of Israel marched through the sea on dry ground, the waters forming a wall for them on their right and on their left.

This is how, on that awesome day, the Lord saved Israel from the hands of the Egyptians. When the Children of Israel saw God's mighty power, they believed in Him, and in the man of God, His faithful servant, Moses.

The Song at the Sea

After Moses and the Children of Israel walked safely through the Sea of Reeds, they sang this song of praise to God:

I will sing to the Lord for He has triumphed.
Horses and riders He has hurled into the sea.
The Lord is my strength,
The Lord has saved me,
The Lord is my God
And my father's God before me.
The Lord has fought for justice,
He has made His children free.
Pharaoh's chariots and armies
He hurled into the sea.
Pharaoh's finest soldiers
Into the Sea of Reeds were thrown,
Hundreds upon hundreds tossed
And tumbled like a stone.
Your right hand had the power,

135

Oh Lord, to break the foe.
Beneath the sea
They sank like lead
When Your wind began to blow.
Who is like You, God on high,
Who is like You, God so holy,
With awesome deeds and wonders,
Who is like You, God on high?
Fear and dread
Conquered all,
Your power made the enemy fall.
Soon the day will come
When Your people reach the land,
The land of milk and honey
That You promised with Your hand.
All of Pharaoh's horses
Went into the sea,
His chariots and his riders
Went into the sea,
The Lord turned back the waters
And beneath the sea they drowned,
But the Children of Israel
Marched upon dry ground.
Then Miriam, Aaron's sister,
Took her tambourine in hand
And said to all the women
Who had marched upon dry land,
"Follow me
And take your tambourines."
They danced as Miriam sang
This song of praise and victory:
Sing unto the Lord
For He has triumphed greatly;
Horses and riders
He has hurled into the sea!

How the Lord Fed His People

Moses led the Children of Israel onward, away from the Sea of Reeds. For three days, the long caravan traveled into the wilderness. This was a gloomy part of the land, full of lizards and snakes who lived under the few scrubby trees and prickly bushes. It was very dry there, and everyone was thirsty. When they reached Marah, the first rest stop, they found bitter water, salty and undrinkable. The people were grumbling. They complained to Moses, "What shall we drink?" Moses asked God for help. The Lord showed Moses how to sweeten the water by throwing a certain kind of wood into it. It worked like magic! Bitter water became sweet!

After everyone drank their fill, the Lord gave His people some special rules to obey. He said, "If you will listen carefully to the Lord your God, and do what is right in His eyes, obey His commandments and follow His laws, then I will not bring upon you any of the diseases that I brought upon the Egyptians, for I, the Lord, am your healer."

The Children of Israel's next stop was a beautiful place called Elim. There were twelve springs of water and seventy palm trees.

This was wonderful! Everyone needed a rest, including the camels and donkeys who had been carrying big loads and pulling heavy carts. After helping to unload the animals,

The children ran in
And ran out of the water,
Splashing and kicking,
Dunking and squirting.
The camels were slurping,
And water was dripping
Down their hairy old chins
Onto chickens and ducks
Who had the good luck to be
Under their legs at the time.
The grown-ups felt sweaty,
And grubby and grimy;
They began washing dirt
From faces and feet.
When their scrubbing was done
And their flocks had been fed,
They lay under the palm trees
And fell fast asleep.

After this peaceful pause in their journey, the Israelites moved on to another barren wilderness called Sin. It had been one month since they left Egypt, and food was running low. Again they began to grumble and complain to Moses and Aaron. They said, "If only we had died by the hand of the Lord in Egypt, where we had wonderful food and delicious bread. You have brought us to this awful, empty wilderness to starve us to death!"

The Lord, who heard everything, said to Moses, "I will send food down to you like the rain from heaven. The people shall go out each day and gather what they need. This is one way that I will test them to see if they follow My instructions. On the sixth day, they will see that what they have gathered is twice the usual amount, enough to feed them through the Sabbath, when no work is to be done."

Moses and Aaron said to the Children of Israel, "This evening, you shall know that it was the Lord who brought you out from the land of Egypt. And in the morning, you shall see the Glory of God, for He has heard your grumbling. You think you are grumbling against us, but you are really questioning God!"

Moses told Aaron to tell all the people, "Come before the Lord, for He has heard your grumbling."

As Aaron spoke, the Children of Israel turned toward the wilderness and saw a huge cloud, shining with a glorious light. The Lord spoke to Moses and said, "I have heard the people's complaints. Tell them: By nighttime, you shall have a good meal and in the morning you shall also have your share of food; and you shall know that I am the Lord!"

That very evening, thousands of quails appeared. Quails are small birds, like pigeons, that fly with the wind. When they get tired flapping their wings, they are easily captured by hand. The Children of Israel caught many quails that night and they ate well, just as the Lord had promised.

The next morning, a layer of dew covered the whole camp. As the sun began to peek over the hills, it evaporated, leaving a fine, flaky substance, delicate as frost, on the ground and bushes. It was white, like spicy coriander seeds, and it tasted like thin crackers made with honey. When the Israelites saw this, they were astonished! Looking at each other they asked, "What is it?"

Moses replied, "It is the food that the Lord has given you to eat. This is what God has commanded: Each of you gather as much as you need, according to the number of people in your tent."

The people did as they were told; some gathered more and some gathered less. Then Moses said, "No one is to leave any of this food for the morning."

But some of the Israelites paid no attention to Moses. They did not have faith that God would provide the next day's meal, and so they kept some of it overnight. In the morning, the leftovers were full of worms and smelled terrible. Moses did not like being disobeyed and was very, very angry. After all, he was trying his best to do as God commanded and help the Children of Israel reach the Promised Land. In their hearts, the Israelites knew this, and they began to listen better. So they gathered the miraculous food early every morning, before the hot sun caused it to melt, each person according to daily needs.

On the sixth day, they seemed to gather twice as much food. When the leaders of the people told Moses about this he said to them, "This is what the Lord meant by the extra portion. Tomorrow is a day of rest and holiness, a Sabbath of the Lord. Bake what you need to bake and boil what you need to boil. Put aside whatever you have left and keep it till the morning." They put it aside, as Moses directed, and it did not get wormy or smelly.

The following morning Moses said, "Eat the leftover food today. Since this is the Lord's Sabbath, you will not find any more food out on the plain. You may gather it in for six days, but on the seventh day there will be none."

Some of the people disobeyed God's orders and went out to try and find the mysterious food. But there was none. The Lord said to Moses, "How long will your people refuse to obey My com-

mandments and My teachings? I have given you the Sabbath. This is very important! On the sixth day I give you enough food for two days. Let no man leave his place on the seventh day!''

This time the people listened to the word of God. They rested and did not gather food on the seventh day.

The Lord fed the Children of Israel His special, miraculous food for forty years, until they entered the Promised Land.

The Israelites were slowly learning God's rules. However, at times these people could be exasperating. When the Lord directed Moses to lead them to Rephidim, the next stop on their trip, they could find no water to drink. The people kicked up a fuss, quarreled with Moses, and cried, ''Give us water to drink!''

Moses was really upset! In a loud voice he said, ''Why do you quarrel with me? Why are you trying the Lord's patience?''

But the people were thirsty, and once again they grumbled and complained, ''Why have you brought us up from Egypt to kill us and our cattle and our children with thirst?''

142

That was it! Moses threw his hands up! He cried to the Lord, "What shall I do with these people? They are almost ready to stone me!"

The Lord, in His kind and calm way, told Moses, "Go to the people and take some of their leaders with you to witness a wonder that I will perform. Take in your hand the rod with which you struck the river. I will stand before you on the rock up in Horeb. Strike the rock and water will flow from it." Together, Moses and Aaron did as the Lord commanded.

Down, down, down flowed the water,
Down from the rock of the Lord.
It seemed as though a well had burst
As the Children of Israel quenched their thirst.
Although they quarreled and tested,
Although they were slow to obey,
God forgave His children
And helped them find their way
Up, up, up to the land,
Up to the land of the Lord,
Where fig trees bloom and olives grow,
Where the nights are cool and soft winds blow,
Up in the land of the Lord.

The Voice of God

Once a month, the moon wakes up with the sun, and the two great lights travel together across the sky. On this special day, the moon's sunlit face is hidden from the earth. The night is dark; the stars miss their companion. This is called the New Moon.

On the day of the third New Moon after the Israelites had left Egypt, they entered the wilderness of Sinai. The camels and donkeys were unloaded and camp was set up in front of the Mountain of God. As soon as he could, Moses went up to talk with his best friend, the Lord. God called down to Moses and said, "Tell this to the women who teach our traditions to the young, and to all the Children of Israel: you have seen what I did to the Egyptians. Now if you will listen to My voice and keep My covenant, you shall be My special treasure among all peoples. You shall be a kingdom of priests and take care of the rest of the world. You shall be a holy nation."

Like the mother eagle who carries her baby on her shoulders to protect it from the hunter's arrows, the great power of God protected the Children of Israel and brought them to Him.

Moses came down from the mountain, summoned the leaders of the people, and told them what God had said. All the people answered as one and said, "We will do as the Lord has told us."

After Moses related the people's words to Him, the Lord said, "I will come to you in a thick, dark cloud. The people will hear My voice when I speak to you, and this way they will always believe you. Go to the people and prepare them to meet God. Have them wash their clothes and bodies in this clear mountain stream. Tell them to purify themselves for the third day, because on that day the Lord will come down, in the sight of all the people, onto Mount Sinai. Tell them they may not go anywhere near the mountain till they hear a long, wailing blast from a ram's horn."

Moses told the Children of Israel what to do. They followed his orders and waited nervously, in great anticipation for the third day to arrive.

On the morning of the third day, great clashes of thunder and flashes of lightning awakened the sleeping Israelites. A thick, dark cloud clung to the mountain, hiding the Divine Presence of God. The loud wail of the ram's horn pierced the air. The people trembled. It was an awesome day!

Moses led the people out of the camp to meet God. They stood at the foot of the mountain and looked up. Mount Sinai was covered with smoke; the Lord had come down upon it in fire. The smoke rose like the smoke of a furnace; the whole mountain shook violently as the wailing of the ram's horn grew louder and louder!

The Lord came down upon the top of Mount Sinai and called for Moses to come up to Him. He told Moses to be sure that the people did not come up the mountain. Moses replied, "The people will not come up because You warned them not to."

The Lord said, "Go down and come back with your brother, Aaron." Again, He repeated His warning to Moses not to let the people break through and gaze upon God. If that happened, they would all have to be destroyed. Moses, God's faithful servant, did as he was told.

Suddenly, from the top of the mountain, a mighty voice was heard! It soared over the crashing thunder and drowned out the

wail of the ram's horn! This was the voice of God! He said, "I AM
THE LORD."

THE SILENT WORLD

The world was wrapped in silence.
Singing birds were still,
Butterflies in mid-flight paused,
Suspended in the sun.
Everyone stopped talking,
Poppies bowed their heads in awe,
And the soft wind held its breath
When God gave Israel His Law.

The Ten Commandments

1. I am the Lord your God, who brought you out of the land of Egypt, out of the house of bondage.

The most important thing about God is to believe in His existence. He is, was, and always will be God, the only God. He is the God of Freedom Who, by working His miracles, rescued a great nation from evil hands.

2. You shall have no other gods beside Me.

The Children of Israel are not allowed to pray to anyone except God. The Children of Israel are not allowed to worship statues or sculptures of anything in

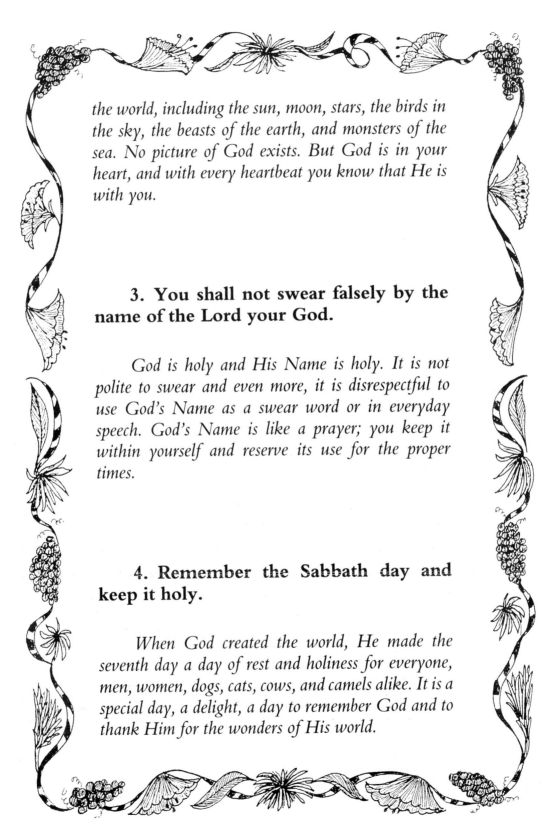

the world, including the sun, moon, stars, the birds in the sky, the beasts of the earth, and monsters of the sea. No picture of God exists. But God is in your heart, and with every heartbeat you know that He is with you.

3. You shall not swear falsely by the name of the Lord your God.

God is holy and His Name is holy. It is not polite to swear and even more, it is disrespectful to use God's Name as a swear word or in everyday speech. God's Name is like a prayer; you keep it within yourself and reserve its use for the proper times.

4. Remember the Sabbath day and keep it holy.

When God created the world, He made the seventh day a day of rest and holiness for everyone, men, women, dogs, cats, cows, and camels alike. It is a special day, a delight, a day to remember God and to thank Him for the wonders of His world.

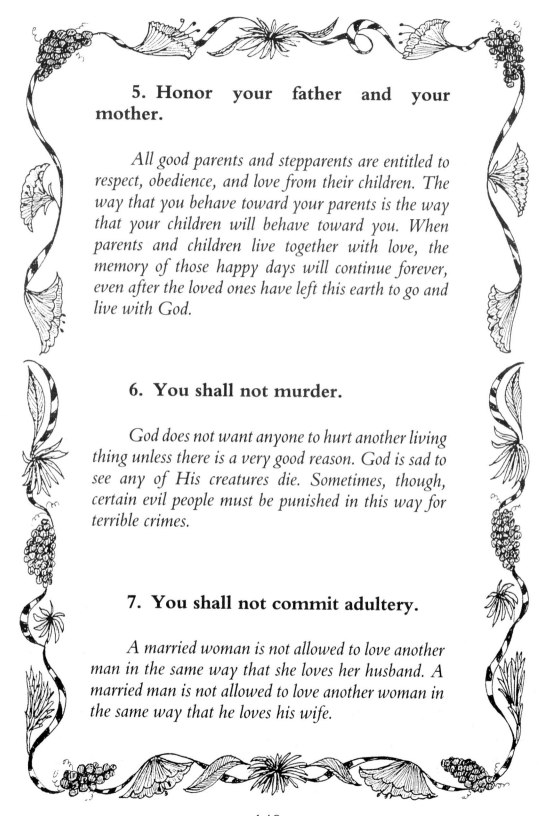

5. Honor your father and your mother.

All good parents and stepparents are entitled to respect, obedience, and love from their children. The way that you behave toward your parents is the way that your children will behave toward you. When parents and children live together with love, the memory of those happy days will continue forever, even after the loved ones have left this earth to go and live with God.

6. You shall not murder.

God does not want anyone to hurt another living thing unless there is a very good reason. God is sad to see any of His creatures die. Sometimes, though, certain evil people must be punished in this way for terrible crimes.

7. You shall not commit adultery.

A married woman is not allowed to love another man in the same way that she loves her husband. A married man is not allowed to love another woman in the same way that he loves his wife.

149

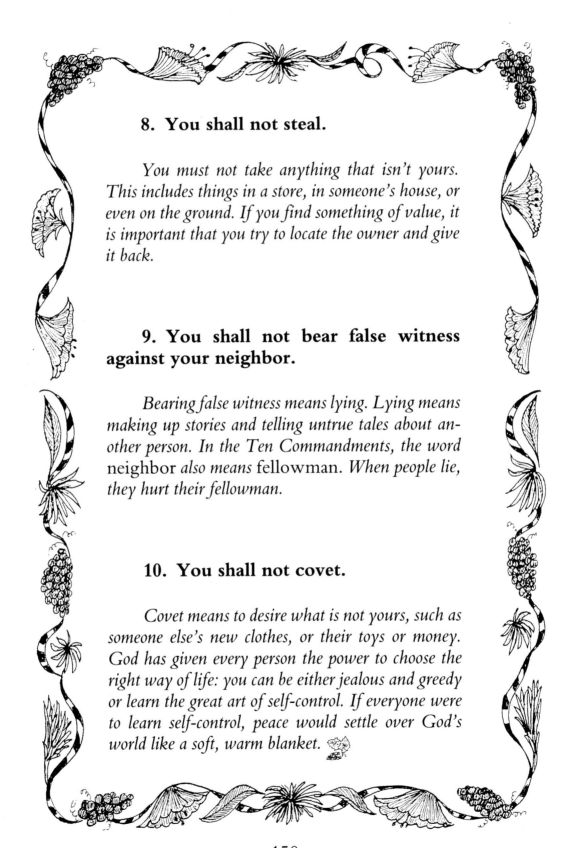

8. You shall not steal.

You must not take anything that isn't yours. This includes things in a store, in someone's house, or even on the ground. If you find something of value, it is important that you try to locate the owner and give it back.

9. You shall not bear false witness against your neighbor.

Bearing false witness means lying. Lying means making up stories and telling untrue tales about another person. In the Ten Commandments, the word neighbor *also means* fellowman. *When people lie, they hurt their fellowman.*

10. You shall not covet.

Covet means to desire what is not yours, such as someone else's new clothes, or their toys or money. God has given every person the power to choose the right way of life: you can be either jealous and greedy or learn the great art of self-control. If everyone were to learn self-control, peace would settle over God's world like a soft, warm blanket.

The Story of the Golden Calf

The Children of Israel were trembling with fear and amazement. They had heard booming crashes of thunder, witnessed blinding lightning flashes, been frightened by the loud blaring of the ram's horn, and were absolutely astonished to see all the smoke coming from the mountaintop! They stood back, afraid to move an inch! After telling the people to return to their tents and be calm, Moses once again approached the thick, dark cloud, the Cloud of God.

The Lord said to Moses, "Tell this to the Israelites: You yourselves saw with your own eyes that I spoke to you from above. Therefore, you shall not make any gods of silver or gold! I will teach you to make Me the proper kind of altar for worship. And I will bless you, wherever you may be when My Name is mentioned." God then gave Moses all the rules and laws that His people, the Children of Israel, were to learn and obey.

It is important to listen carefully when you are taught new things. Because Moses listened carefully to God, he was able to repeat to the people in the camp all that he had heard. After listening to the rules and laws, the people answered together, "All the things that the Lord has commanded we will do."

151

Early in the morning, as the sun was pulling itself sleepily over the horizon, Moses, following God's directions, built an altar at the foot of the mountain. He also erected twelve pillars, one for each of the twelve tribes of Israel. Some of the younger men were given the honor of making burnt offerings and peace offerings of oxen to the Lord. After performing certain rituals in front of the altar, Moses took the Book of the Covenant, the laws and rules of God, and read it to the people. They again promised, "All that the Lord has said we will do and obey."

Moses then said, "This ceremony makes God and the Children of Israel partners forever."

The Lord said to Moses, "Come up to Me on the mountain and wait. I will give you stone tablets with the teachings and commandments that I have written in order to teach these people."

Moses and Joshua, Moses' young helper, climbed cautiously over rocks and prickly bushes and began to make their way slowly up the Mountain of God. As he was leaving, Moses told the older leaders of Israel, "Wait here for us till we return. You have Aaron and his friend Hur with you. If there are any problems, consult them. They are in charge."

The great cloud once again covered the top of the mountain. This was the Presence of the Lord. Down in the camp, the Presence of the Lord looked like a blazing fire on top of the mountain. These events were becoming more and more mysterious to the Children of Israel.

For six days Mount Sinai was hidden by the gigantic cloud. On the seventh day, the Lord called to Moses from the midst of the cloud. Moses was not afraid. He had great faith in God, his very best friend. Leaving Joshua behind, Moses went inside the cloud and continued up the mountain. And he stayed on the Mountain of God for forty days and forty nights.

While Moses was with the Lord, the Children of Israel went about their daily chores. But as the days went by, and Moses did not return, they began to worry. They felt alone and abandoned. Who would lead them out of this wilderness? Where was this man, Moses? Why was he taking so long to come back to them? Was he dead? Some of them began to lose their faith!

Some people find that waiting is a very hard thing to do. They lose patience and get jumpy, and they lose their tempers, too.

A group of people in the camp
Broke their promise to the Lord.
They forgot the rules
And begged Aaron to make
A god from golden jewels.
Aaron tried to calm them down,
To gain some time, to wait.
Every minute counted and Moses was so late
In coming down from the mountain hidden in the cloud.
But this group was in a tizzy,
A very rowdy crowd
Who gave Aaron all their earrings!

153

Impatience made them loud!
So Aaron made a wooden mold.
He poured the melted gold inside.
With carving tools he made a calf,
And the sinful people cried,
"This is your god,
Oh Israel,
Which brought you up from Pharaoh's land!"
They were worshiping a golden calf made by Aaron's hand!
Aaron didn't argue, he tried to keep the peace.
But he wished that Moses would come down.
He needed some relief!
Perhaps tomorrow!
So he said, "Tomorrow,
In the morning,
We shall have a feast,
A feast unto the Lord and not unto this golden beast!"
Aaron looked up toward the mountain.
He was terribly concerned
About his brother, but tomorrow came
And Moses still had not returned.
As the birds began to sing
Their first good mornings to the sun,
The people ate and danced and drank,
Enjoying all the fun!
They made offerings and brought sacrifices
To the golden calf!
And they did this on the altar
Aaron built in its behalf!
From the mountaintop God saw this,
He was angry and dismayed,
He told Moses, "Hurry,
Go down right away.
Your people whom you lead
Are acting sinfully today.
They are stiff-necked, they have turned aside,

They've disobeyed My rules.
Unless you've got a good excuse
I will destroy these fools!"
But Moses begged the Lord and said,
"Please don't use Your mighty hand
Against Your people whom You alone
Brought out of Egypt land!
Don't let the Egyptians say that God
Delivered and then killed them!
Turn from anger and forget Your plans
To punish and destroy them!
Remember Abraham and Isaac,
Remember Jacob, too,
And Your promise to these good men
That their offspring would be numbered
As the stars that shine in heaven.
Remember that you promised them
A safe and happy land!"
God listened
And gave up the dreadful punishment He'd planned!

Moses was relieved. He came down from the mountain carrying the two tablets of the covenant, written on both sides. The tablets were God's work and the writing was God's writing cut into the stone of the tablets. Joshua, who had been patiently waiting, met Moses on his way down. He said, "There is a cry of war in the camp!" But Moses, who already knew the bad news, said:

> *"It is not the blare of trumpets,*
> *Or the sad tune of defeat.*
> *It is the sound of song, a tribute*
> *To the golden calf at their feet!"*

As Moses came near the camp, he saw the calf and the people eating, drinking, and dancing. He was outraged! This unruly mob of people was unworthy of the great gift that he had brought down from the mountain! He took the tablets that contained the Ten

Commandments, written by the hand of God, and threw them on the ground! They shattered into a million pieces! He took the golden calf, burned it, ground it into a fine powder, and dumped it into the stream that flowed from the mountain. And then he made the Children of Israel drink the bitter, gold-colored water!

Moses was very surprised at Aaron's behavior. He could not believe that Aaron had actually made the golden calf and he demanded an explanation. "What have these people done to you that you have brought this great sin upon them?"

Aaron answered, "Don't be angry. What could I do? It's the people's fault. Some of them are always ready to do bad things. They said to me, 'Make us a god to lead us because we don't know what has happened to that man, Moses, who brought us from the land of Egypt.' I said to them, 'Whoever has gold, take it off!' I thought that would stop them, that they wouldn't give up their fine jewelry. But they tore off their earrings and gave them all to me. So I hurled all of it into the fire and out came this calf! Just like that!"

What a poor excuse! What a story! Aaron put the whole blame on others. And he did not tell the truth! When someone is chosen to be a leader, he must try his best to be worthy of the job. A good leader is always responsible for what his group does. And a good leader always takes the blame for any wrongdoing.

Moses saw that Aaron had let the people get out of control. When the Israelites left Egypt, some other groups decided to tag along. Moses allowed this because most of them seemed to be good people also trying to escape from Pharaoh. But there were hotheads among them looking to make trouble. Some of the Israelites were easily influenced by them, and some of the Israelites just lost their faith, all by themselves. No group of people is ever perfect. Sometimes, in difficult situations, it's the loudmouth who gets his or her way. And this does not always mean that the outcome will be good!

Moses stood at the gate of the camp and said, "Whoever had no part in this and is for the Lord, come here!"

All the sons of Levi came to him.

Moses said, "The Lord has ordered you to put on your swords

156

and slay all the criminals and their relatives, everyone who did this terrible thing." Three thousand people were executed for their crime against God!

Then Moses said, "Dedicate yourself today to the Lord, for in carrying out His orders you too have fought against others. By doing this, by pledging yourself to God, you will again have the privilege of worshiping Him."

The Israelites were ashamed. They had seen the anger of the Lord, and many had been gravely punished. Little children put themselves to bed, and the grown-ups sat around without telling their usual bad jokes. Even the animals were quiet; not one of them snorted or howled, clucked or mooed. All their ears flopped over and their tails hung very low.

The Presence of God

The worst troublemakers in the Israelites' camp had paid for their sin against God with their lives. Moses said to the rest of the Children of Israel, "Although your lives have been spared, you still have all been guilty of a great sin. I will once again go up to the Lord; maybe I'll win forgiveness for this terrible thing that you have done."

Moses went back up to the Lord and said, "These people are guilty of a great sin in allowing the making of that god of gold. If You will forgive them their sin, well and good; but if not, erase me from Your Book of Life." Moses lived for his people. If they were destroyed, he felt his life would be over.

And the Lord said to Moses, "I will only erase from My Book of Life the people who have sinned against Me." The Lord would not permit Moses to suffer for the sins of his people.

"Go now," said the Lord. "Continue to lead the people onward. Since I cannot forget what they have done, I will not go with you this time. But I will send my angel along to help you. However, when I am ready, I will make them pay for their sins!"

Moses was still furious with the Israelites. When he came

down from the mountain he took a large tent and set it up outside the camp. This was called the Tent of Meeting. It was here that Moses would now meet with God and speak to Him face to face. When Moses left the camp and went to the Tent, all the people stood up with respect. When he went into the Tent, a great pillar of cloud blocked the entrance. When the people saw the pillar of cloud, they bowed down to the ground in reverence. The Children of Israel were finally learning how to behave properly.

During their talks, Moses begged God to come with him on his journey to the Promised Land. He told God not to bother sending the people onward if His Presence did not come with them. And God agreed, once again, to lead the Children of Israel.

But Moses still had one more special request. He dared to ask God to show him His Glory, the sacred qualities that made Him God, the Lord! God answered Moses with these words, "I will reveal Myself to you but you cannot see My face, for man cannot see Me and live! There is a place that you will find nearby, on Mount Sinai. Stand there. As My Presence passes by, I will put you in a hollowed-out part of the rock and protect you with My hand till I have passed by. Then I will take My hand away, and you will see My back; but My face must not be seen!"

Then the Lord said to Moses, "Carve two tablets of stone like the first ones. I will write upon the tablets the words that were on the ones that you shattered. Have this ready by morning. Then come up to Me on the mountaintop. No one else must come up with you, and no one else must be seen anywhere on the mountain. Also, the flocks and herds must not graze at the foot of the mountain." The Lord had given His orders. Moses, his faithful friend, obeyed them without a question.

Moses spent the night carving the two tablets of stone. In the early morning, carrying the two heavy tablets, he made his way slowly up to Mount Sinai.

The Lord came down upon the mountaintop in a cloud. He stood there and proclaimed the name "The Lord." The Lord passed by Moses and again proclaimed, "The Lord! The Lord! A God compassionate and gracious, slow to anger, abounding in kindness and faithfulness, extending kindness to the thousandth generation, forgiving wicked acts, evil-doing, and sin; yet He will not allow the guilty to go unpunished, but will inflict punishment for the wicked acts of the people to their families up until the third and fourth generations."

Moses quickly bowed low to the ground in great respect and said, "If I have gained Your favor, O Lord, please come into our midst, even though this is a stiff-necked people. Pardon our wicked acts and our sins, and take us for Your own!"

God then made a sacred pact, a new covenant with the Children of Israel. He described all the wondrous deeds that He would perform and again gave Moses a set of rules and laws to learn. When He was finished, the Lord said to Moses, "Write down these commandments, for with these commandments I make a covenant, a sacred pact with you and with Israel."

Moses stayed with the Lord another forty days and forty nights. He ate no bread and drank no water and he wrote down, on the heavy stone tablets, the sacred covenant, the Ten Commandments.

A GLORIOUS LIGHT

Moses came down from Mount Sinai
With the two tablets of stone.
He had no idea that the skin of his face was
So radiant,
So bright,
That it shone
Like God's Presence,
A glorious light!
When the Israelites looked upon Moses
They were awestruck, they would not come near.
Moses called to them gently,
And when they appeared,
Gave instructions
For all to hear.

160

He read them the rules,
He read them the laws,
That were written on tablets of stone.
If they learned and obeyed them,
And did not betray them,
The Lord God would soon lead them home.

The Tabernacle

When the Lord God forgave the Children of Israel for their great sin, He gave orders to begin building the Tabernacle. This was to be a portable tent that would hold, in a beautiful chest called the Ark, the Tablets of the Law—the Ten Commandments. In this way, God's Presence would travel along with the Israelites as they continued on their journey to the Promised Land.

Soon after coming down from Mount Sinai, Moses gathered the whole community together for a meeting. They listened carefully to his words. First he reminded them about the laws of the Sabbath, the day of rest and holiness. Since this was God's special day, the Lord wanted to be absolutely sure that His people would observe it properly. Then Moses gave the Children of Israel God's instructions for building the Tabernacle:

Take from among you gifts to the Lord,
Silver and copper and gold,
Yarns of crimson, of purple and blue,
Fine woven linen and goat's hair, too.

162

Bring animal skins and acacia wood
And oil for the six-branched lamps,
Incense, spices, and jewels,
And all who have tools must help
The fine craftsmen who work in this camp
Build the great Tabernacle
And its sacred Ark,
Crowned in gold like the sun at dawn.
They'll carve wood for the poles
To carry the sanctuary
With them as they travel on.
They must weave special clothes
For the high priests to wear
When they enter the holiest places.
The people opened their hearts,
Brought gifts to the Lord,
And smiles returned to their faces.

God appointed the Israelites' finest craftsman, Bezalel, to be chief designer of the Tabernacle. Part of his job was to teach the other craftspeople how to cut the twelve precious stones, one for each tribe of Israel, that Aaron, the high priest, would wear over his heart. He also taught them wood carving and how to weave the blue, purple, and scarlet veil that would divide the Tent of Meeting from the Holy of Holies, the place where the Ark rested.

Bezalel made the Ark out of acacia wood and covered it inside and out with pure gold. For the top, Bezalel designed a golden crown with two cherubs, one on either side, their shining wings spread protectively over the sacred Ark. Gold rings and bars were made to hold the Tabernacle together. A colorful, woven screen for the gate and rain covers and carrying poles for traveling were completed. Finally the Tabernacle was finished!

The Lord said to Moses, "Bring Aaron and his sons to the entrance of this Tent of Meeting, the Tabernacle. After they are washed, have Aaron put on the high priest's clothing and anoint him with the sweet-scented oil so that he may serve Me. Then do the same for his sons. This anointing shall make them a family of priests forever."

Moses was now ready to assemble the finished Tabernacle. All the collapsible parts fit together perfectly! He took the stone tablets of the Ten Commandments, placed them gently in the Ark, and carried the Ark inside the Tabernacle. Moses then arranged the interior of the Tabernacle, according to God's orders. He made offerings to the Lord and filled the air with the spicy scent of burning incense.

Building the Tabernacle was a big job. It took lots of effort and hard work to get it finished. But mostly it took cooperation. Learning to work peacefully together on a project can make all the difference in the world. The Children of Israel worked peacefully together and built a beautiful home for the Presence of God. The Lord was very pleased.

After Moses put the last piece in place, God covered the Tent of Meeting with His great, dark cloud. The flowers in the fields lifted their faces; something was about to happen! Earthworms uncurled themselves, dogs lay down with their heads on their paws, and

164

the crickets were silent. From far, far away the sweet singing of angels could be heard. And then the Glorious Presence of the Lord filled the Tabernacle!

When the cloud lifted, the Children of Israel
Carried the Ark toward the Promised land.
And when it did not lift, they rested and waited
Until God was ready to show them His hand.

Leviticus

ויקרא

The Sacrifices

The Children of Israel were busy. Now that the Tabernacle was completed, it was time to pack up the camp and continue on their journey. They took down their tents, folded laundry, looked for lost sandals, and made sure that all the campfires were out. The younger children gathered together the flocks of spotted sheep and long-haired goats, and teenagers listened for cowbells and rounded up the herds of cattle. Everyone

169

tried to catch the little chicks and fuzzy ducklings and return them to their parents for safekeeping during the trip. Strong men and women helped push the sleepy camels upright. Once again, floppy-eared donkeys were loaded up with pots, water jugs, and dishes. Their carts were filled with blankets to make the ride comfortable for mothers, babies, and small children, and especially for grandfathers and grandmothers. Being kind and thoughtful toward elderly people is one of the most important ways to please God and to thank Him for His gift of life.

Aaron the high priest and his sons, who were in charge of taking care of the Tabernacle, were patiently waiting for Moses to give them directions about how to transport the beautiful Sanctuary. However, the great, gray cloud was still over the Tabernacle; the Lord was not quite ready to have the long caravan leave. He called to Moses from inside the Tabernacle and Moses went in, under the great, gray cloud, to hear what God had to say. There were certain instructions that God wanted the Children of Israel to follow: the rules for living a good religious life, how to govern the community with justice and fairness, and certain regulations regarding sacrifices.

In those days, the offering of sacrifices was the way people worshiped God. The Lord provided His children with different kinds of flocks, herds, and crops. They, in turn, brought gifts of these blessings back to God. When a person felt guilty about doing a bad deed, he would bring God a sacrifice and promise to behave better in the future. Sometimes, if a person wanted to thank God for something nice or to fulfill a promise he or she made, a peace-offering sacrifice would be given. A sin-offering sacrifice would be made to apologize to God for an accidental wrongdoing and to ask His forgiveness. It did not matter how big or small the sacrifice was; even a tiny bit of grain would please the Lord if it were offered with the hope of coming closer to God.

By offering sacrifices, the Israelites felt that they were able to clean away their sins and clear their guilty consciences. Nowadays, sacrifice has been replaced by our gift of prayer and good deeds. The more we pray and the nicer we behave toward our fellow men and women, the closer we get to the Presence of God.

PRAYERS

A prayer of thanks in the morning
As we open up our eyes and see
The sunshine peeking over
Our soft pillow and our sheet.
And then a breakfast prayer of thanks
Before we eat
Our cereal or scrambled eggs,
Juice and milk or tea.
All through the day we thank the Lord
For the things we need to live
A healthy and a happy life
Of kindness and good deeds.
But if it happens that we do a wrong,
Or say a nasty word,
Then we can pray and know
That God will listen to us, and forgive.
A prayer of thanks when the sun goes down
And the moon turns on its light,
"Let me lie down this night in peace;
I shall not be afraid.
Let Your angels gently close my eyes
And sing their lullabies."

171

You Shall Be Holy

Most new babies come into the world kicking and yelling, happy to be alive! When they are picked up and held close to their mother's heart, they calm down and learn to be quiet. This is a child's first lesson. Because the Lord God created His people, He wanted the Children of Israel to think of this gift of life as sacred. Since the Israelites were like newly born children, just beginning to learn rules and laws, God had to teach them how to behave. The Lord spoke to Moses and said, "Speak to the whole Israelite community and tell them: You must be holy, because I, the Lord, am holy." And then He gave Moses the Laws of Holiness, a set of rules that told His people how He expected them to live their lives. To be close with God, everyone must try to follow these Laws of Holiness:

"You must respect your mother and your father,
And always be polite,
Remember, parents once were children, too,
And they try to do what's right.
You must keep My Holy Sabbath

172

As a day of rest and peace.
You must not make gods of gold or stone,
For I, the Lord, am God, alone.
When you cut the harvest of your land
Let the fallen wheat be left
In kindness for the hungry,
To provide them food to eat.
You must pay your workers promptly,
Don't keep their money overnight.
You must not insult the hard of hearing
Or trip the one who has no sight.
No matter if they're rich or poor
Treat all people the same.
And don't tell tales or gossip,
Or call anybody names.
Try to make friends with your enemies

And don't stand idly by
While someone is in trouble:
You must not let another die!
Be nice to foreign people
Though their language may be odd,
Remember—you were strangers too, in Egypt,
I, the Lord, am God!
When you are kind, and show compassion,
When you are merciful and wise,
And love your neighbor as yourself,
You will be holy in God's eyes."

Numbers

במדבר

Ready To Leave

By the second year after the Exodus from Egypt, the huge caravan of Israelites was becoming more and more orderly. God had taught them rules and laws, and the people were behaving better. With a little help and some practice, everybody, young and old, can improve themselves.

Everyone was packed up and ready to continue the journey. But God wanted to make sure that His people were organized correctly. It is not good to rush into big projects without detailed plans. Moving so many people and animals was a very big project and God didn't want anyone to get lost. So the Lord spoke to Moses from inside the beautiful Tabernacle and said, "Count all the Children of Israel, tribe by tribe and family by family. Also count every male over the age of twenty. These men will be your army and defend you as you travel. Take one special man from each of the twelve tribes to help you do the counting."

Moses, Aaron, and the twelve men counted six hundred and three thousand, five hundred and fifty able-bodied men. Only the Levites were not among those chosen to be soldiers; the Lord wanted them to be the caretakers of the Tabernacle.

177

The next part of the Lord's plan was to assemble the Children of Israel into easily managed groups. He told Moses and Aaron, "Tell the Israelites to pitch their tents by the flags of their own tribes."

When this announcement was made, the great crowd scurried around like thousands of ants, looking every which way for each family's flag. The camp of Judah was on the east side, toward the rising sun. Next to Judah were the camps of Issachar and Zebulun. These three tribes would be the first to move forward. The flag of the camp of Reuben was raised on the south side, along with the flags of Simeon and Gad. They would be the second group to march. The Levites were to remain in the middle; God wanted His Tabernacle to always be in the center of the Children of Israel. The tribes of Ephraim and Manasseh, who were the descendants of Joseph, and the tribe of Benjamin gathered on the west side. These people would follow the Levites. On the north side stood the flags of Dan, Asher, and Naphtali. These three tribes would be the last to leave.

What a job! But since the Children of Israel were now listening carefully to instructions, only a few people and a big old goose got mixed up. Everyone helped their neighbors, and people soon found their proper places. The children of each tribe tied colored ribbons on their donkeys' ears for identification. When the camels decided to lie down and relax again, name tags were attached to their humps. Soon, the whole camp was in order. As the bright flags waved in the desert breeze, the Children of Israel waited patiently for directions. It was almost time to leave.

The Levites had been given strict rules about taking down and setting up the Tabernacle: the boards, rods, rings, furniture, altars, curtains, and beautiful woven tapestries were to be placed on six covered wagons, each pulled by two very strong oxen. The most sacred objects, the Ark and the menorah, were to be carried carefully on the men's shoulders.

The Children of Israel were reminded to watch for the Lord's signs: When the great, gray cloud rose above the Tabernacle, they would be allowed to go forward. But when the cloud covered the

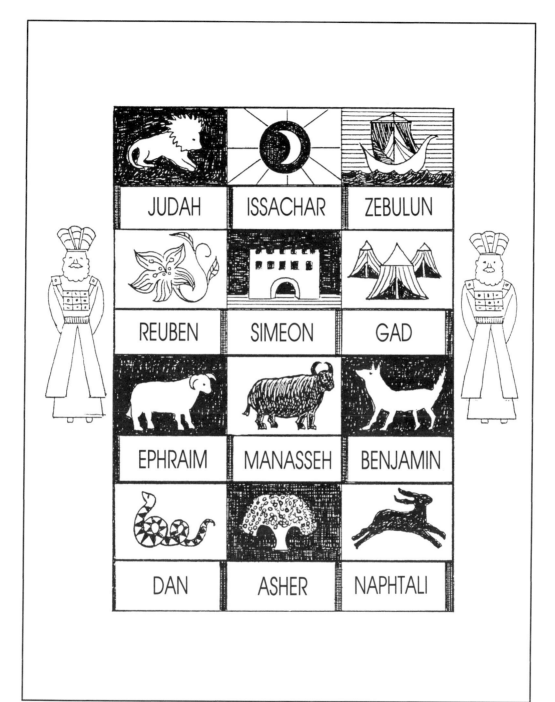

Tabernacle, they would have to set up camp and wait, sometimes only overnight and sometimes for days or even months. Whatever happened, the Israelites were to obey God's commands given to them through Moses.

The Lord gave one last order: two shiny silver trumpets were to be made. Being a trumpet blower was a wonderful and important job. Special signals would call the whole camp together, warn against danger, and tell everyone when to start and stop. The sound of trumpets helped bring courage and cheerfulness to the Children of Israel.

When the Lord God was satisfied that the giant caravan was organized and ready to leave for the Promised Land, He said to Moses, "Here are the words that Aaron and his sons shall use to bless the Children of Israel. Remember them forever:

"The Lord Bless you and keep you.
The Lord make his face to shine upon you and be gracious to you.
The Lord lift up His countenance upon you, and give you peace."

With God's blessing, the Children of Israel finally went forward, out of the wilderness of Sinai, toward the land of milk and honey.

GOD'S BLESSINGS

God blesses us with life and health,
With knowledge and kind ways.
He watches us and gives us love
And guides us through our days.
But most of all He gives to us
His sacred gift of peace,
And if we try to keep peace in our hearts
Then maybe wars will cease.
We should be thoughtful and forgiving,
And we should try hard not to fight
Because the Lord made us to be like Him,
To be wise and do what's right.

Quails

The big camp was very still; something important was about to happen. Children tried not to fidget, donkeys perked up their floppy ears, and the camels stopped their snorting and stomping. Everyone watched as the great, gray cloud slowly lifted up from the Tabernacle. And then the sound of the two silver trumpets echoed back and forth in the air. This was the signal to move forward. As instructed, the Israelites began to march, tribe by tribe, family by family. Since this was the first time that the Ark journeyed, it led the procession, to give the people confidence and courage. From that moment on, every time the Ark traveled, Moses would say, "Give aid, O Lord, and let Your enemies be scattered. And let Your foes flee before You."

A desert is a hot, dry place. It is almost impossible to find any relief from the burning sun. But the Lord God found a way to help the Israelites with this problem: He caused His great, gray cloud to hover over the caravan, like a huge beach umbrella, making it shady and cool for them as they marched out of the wilderness of Sinai.

After three long days and nights of traveling, the trumpet blowers signaled everyone to stop: the cloud once again lay on top

of the Tabernacle. And from that moment on, every time the Ark rested, Moses would say, "Return, O Lord, unto the ten thousands of the families of Israel."

The Children of Israel marched and stopped, marched and stopped, for days and days. The sand was hot, the rocky ground was bumpy, and soon some of the Israelites began to lose their tempers and their faith. They complained about the weather, about their sore feet, about being thirsty, about each other, and most of all they complained about the food:

> *"In Egypt," they said, "we had onions and melons,*
> *Cucumbers and garlic and plenty of leeks.*
> *All that we have here is sweet dew from heaven,*
> *If only we could have some fine meat to eat!"*

Moses heard weeping coming from the tents and did not know what to do. He asked the Lord, "Why have You been so hard on me? What have I done wrong in Your eyes? You have given me the burden of all these people! Did I give birth to them? Am I supposed to carry them in my arms like a father carrying a nursing baby, and bring them to the land that You promised to their fathers? How in the world can I find them meat to eat; they are always crying, 'Give us meat, give us meat.' I cannot take care of these people by myself. It is too heavy a load for me! If this is how You wish to deal with me, then kill me please. I have tried so hard to teach these people and I cannot stand to see my failure!"

It is not easy to always have a good attitude, especially when the people that you try to help do nothing but grumble and complain. Sometimes even the most understanding people, like Moses, become displeased and unhappy.

The Lord answered Moses, "Gather seventy leaders of Israel and bring them with you to the Tent of Meeting. I will give them some of the spirit of leadership that I have given you. In this way they will help share the burden of dealing with all these complainers. You will not have to carry such a heavy load alone. Tell them to say to the people: Tomorrow you shall eat meat, for the Lord has heard you weeping and saying, 'If only we had meat to eat. After all, we remember that in Egypt we had really good food.' Therefore, the Lord will give you meat to eat:

"Not for one day or for two,
Nor five or ten or twenty,
But you shall eat meat for a month
Till it comes out of your noses,
Till you loathe it
And it makes you sick!
This is not what I expected
When I brought you out of Egypt!
My word is not to be rejected!"

Moses was not sure what God meant to do. He said, "There are over six hundred thousand people in this camp and yet You have said, 'I will give them meat to eat for a whole month.' Can enough herds and flocks be slaughtered to feed them? If all the fish in the sea were caught, would that be enough to satisfy them?"

God answered this question with a mighty voice, "Is there a limit to the Lord's power? You shall soon see if My promise comes true or not!"

Moses told the Children of Israel exactly what the Lord had said. Although a good many people were perfectly content with their food, the grumblers and loud complainers could hardly wait to fill their bellies with meat. They were thinking of nothing but their own immediate desires.

And then the Lord God caused a wind to blow
From far across the sea,
And flying with the wind came quails,
Thousands and thousands of little quails,
Covering the sky
As far as any eye could see!
They fell all around the camp
And made a quail pile three feet high!

All that day and night
And all the next day, too,
People gathered heaps of quails.
They were grabbing,
They were eating fast
And gobbling up the quails!
But while the meat was still between their teeth
They gave terrifying wails!
The Lord God had shown His anger,
It came upon them, blazing hot,
And He caused a plague to strike them dead,
Right there on the spot
Where they were chewing all the meat,
And thinking only of their need!
And they were buried in a place their families called
"The Graves of Greed."

The Twelve Spies

An oasis is a cool, green place that appears, almost out of nowhere, in different parts of a hot, dry desert. When the Israelites reached the desert wilderness of Paran, they found the oasis of Kadesh-Barnea. What a relief! They set the camp up around the Tabernacle as they had been taught, fed all the animals, and let the children run around for exercise. There were some nice, big palm trees in this oasis, and in no time people were lying under them on blankets, enjoying the shade. Tired, sore feet were soothed by a little stream that found its way all around the camp. Now, at last, the weary travelers could rest for a while.

Shortly after they arrived, the Lord called Moses to the Tabernacle. He asked Moses to select twelve leading men, one from each tribe, to act as spies. They were to go to Canaan, search it out, and bring back a report. After picking the twelve men, Moses gave them their orders: "Go south, up into the hill country, and see what the land looks like. Find out what kind of people live there, if they are strong or weak, few or many. See if they have cities made of stone or campgrounds with tents. Check and see if the land is fertile or barren, and if there is any wood around. And try very hard to

187

bring back some fruit that may be in season; after all, this is the time for grapes."

The twelve-man team left Kadesh-Barnea and began their spying mission. They went up hills and down valleys, through cracked and dry wilderness and into green, fertile places. Along the way, they saw some big old cities and some big young men. There were many miles to cover, and it took forty days to complete the job. When they finally came back, ready to give Moses the report, they were carrying important evidence: an enormous cluster of purple grapes that hung between a pole carried by two men. Other men carried baskets of pomegranates and figs. Everyone came running to see these marvelous, juicy treats. The spies said to Moses, "The land where you sent us surely flows with milk and honey; here are some of its fruits." That was the good news. The rest of the report was gloomy and frightening. They said:

"There are very strong people
Who live in big cities
With walls all around
For defense and protection.
There are giants among them,
Men of great height,
And fierce mountain people,
Hittites, Jebusites, Amorites.
And the dry land to the south
Is full of Amalekites.
There are Canaanites living
Alongside the water.
If we fight them
We'll be leading our people to slaughter."
But two of the spies,
Named Caleb and Joshua,
Disagreed with the others
And said, "If you please,
We should go into Canaan,
And try to possess it,

188

It's the Lord's Promised Land
And He's ready to bless it."
But the other ten men
Were creating a fuss,
Saying, "The land that we spied on
Could never support us.
And the giants who live there
Are ready to fight.
We must look just like grasshoppers
In their sight!"

That night, the whole camp wept with fear and disappointment. They grumbled and complained and took their anger out on Moses and Aaron. "If only we had died in Egypt or here in this wilderness!" they cried. "Why is the Lord taking us to that land to be killed by fearsome people? Our children will be victims! Maybe we should choose another leader and return to Egypt!"

The people were getting each other excited and worked up. All kinds of rumors spread from tribe to tribe, person to person. Spreading rumors always causes trouble; you never know where the truth stops and the lies begin.

Moses and Aaron were at their wits' end; they did not know whether to feel sorry or ashamed. Two of the spies, Joshua and Caleb, tried their best to calm the angry crowd and change their minds. They told the Children of Israel, "The land that we passed through was good, fertile country. If we please the Lord, He will bring us there safely and give us this country, which is filled with milk and honey. Do not rebel against the Lord and do not fear the people who live there. They will melt away like the sweet dew when the sun is high. The Lord will protect us; do not fear them!"

But the whole camp was in a panic; nobody listened to Joshua and Caleb or took the time to think clearly. Everyone was yelling and screaming; even the animals were howling and bleating and stamping their hooves. The furious crowd was about to stone Moses and Aaron when suddenly, the Glory of the Lord appeared in the Tent of Meeting.

190

Once again, the Lord was full of anger! He said to Moses, "How long will these people continue to provoke Me? In spite of all the wonders that I have shown them, how long will it take for them to trust Me? I will bring disease upon them and they shall be no more! But I shall make you and your children into a great nation, greater than the one I promised to your ancestors!"

Moses then begged the Lord to forgive the Children of Israel. He said, "When the Egyptians hear that You have killed Your people in the wilderness, they will say, 'The Lord did this because He was not able to bring His people into the land that He promised them.' Now, I beg of You, show us Your greatness. You have taught us that the Lord is slow to anger, full of compassion, and that He forgives sins and wrongdoings, although the bad deeds of the guilty will be remembered long after they are gone. I beg You to allow Your great loving-kindness to forgive the sins of these people in the same way that You have forgiven them since they left Egypt!"

FORGIVING

It is often hard to say
"I'm sorry" or "Forgive me."
Sometimes it takes courage
Just to say the words.
Sometimes you feel embarrassed,
And can't look others in the eyes,
And sometimes the other person
Will not let you apologize.
But the Lord God always listens
To our prayers to be forgiven,
His ears are open and His heart
Has lots of room for us to live in.

The Lord said to Moses, "I have pardoned them as you have asked. But as truly as I am the Lord, these people, who have seen My Glory, who have witnessed My signs and wonders that I performed in Egypt and in the wilderness and who still have not listened to My voice, shall not see the land that I promised to their fathers! Tell them that their words will be fulfilled: they will die in the wilderness! Every person, from twenty years of age and up, will not come into the Promised Land! Only Joshua and Caleb, who believed in Me and followed My directions, will be allowed to enter. The rest of them and their children shall wander in the wilderness for forty years, a year for each day that it took to spy on the land. By this punishment, they will know My displeasure!''

Of the twelve spies, the ten men who had started all the trouble by giving the evil report died of a terrible plague. Only Joshua and Caleb remained untouched. When the Children of Israel heard this bad news, they felt terrible and mourned their leaders. In the morning, some of the Israelites went to the top of the nearest mountain and said, "We know that we have sinned. We are now prepared to go into the land that the Lord promised."

Moses said, "Why are you once again disobeying the Lord's command? Don't you dare go up into that land because the Lord will not be with you to protect you from enemies! You will die by their swords!"

But the men would not listen to Moses. They were stubborn and did exactly as they wished. The Ark of the Lord remained in the camp, covered by the great, gray cloud. And the men who would not listen were never seen again.

The Sin of Moses

The Children of Israel wandered forty years
    Until they came into the wilderness of Zin,
    Another desert, hot and dry,
And they were angry and they cried
To Moses and to Aaron,
"Why have you brought us to this evil place
That has no water?
It is barren!"
Moses and his brother
Went into the Tent of Meeting
And fell upon their faces,
This was how they honored God.
The Glory of the Lord appeared
And said to Moses, "Take your rod,
And stand in front of your whining, thirsty camp.
Speak to the rock that you will find there,
And tell it to give water!"
Moses did as he was ordered.
He got the camp assembled,

His impatience showing through, and said,
"Listen, foolish people,
Everyone of you,
Are we to bring water from this rock?"
Moses lifted up his hand
And disobeyed the Lord's command!
Instead of speaking to the rock,
He struck it once!
He struck it twice!
Water poured out!
Water spilled!

194

Man and beast both drank their fill
Until
The Lord told Moses and told Aaron,
"You have gone against My will!
If you had not been impatient,
If you had not doubted Me,
And if you'd spoken to the rock
As I commanded you to do,
Then I would not punish you!
But those who do not listen to Me
Suffer by My hand!
Therefore,
I shall not let either one of you
Into the Promised Land!"

195

The Donkey Who Talked

When Aaron was very old, the Lord told Moses to bring him and his son, Eleazar, up to the top of Mount Hor. The Lord said to Moses, "Aaron shall die here. He shall not enter the land that I have given to the Children of Israel because you both were impatient and doubted my word. Take Aaron's priestly clothes and put them on his son, Eleazar. He will now become the high priest and perform the ceremonies in the Taber-nacle."

Moses and Eleazar walked slowly down the mountain. They could not believe that Aaron was gone forever. It is hard to say good-bye to someone you have known for your entire life, and they were both terribly sad. When the people in the camp heard that Aaron, the man who spoke calmly and tried to keep the peace, had been buried on the mountain, they wept and mourned for thirty days. Everyone missed Aaron.

After forty years, the new generation of Israelites had become good, courageous soldiers. It was now time to move forward, closer to the Promised Land. They were considerate people, and every time they wanted to pass through a new territory, they would let the local king know that they meant no harm. Although they were peaceful, other groups often attacked them. Because they were young and brave, the Children of Israel fought back and won many battles. Stories about their victories soon were heard in all the different countries that bordered Canaan. As their reputation grew, so did other people's fears.

Balak, the king of Moab, had heard these stories; some were tall tales and some were true. He began to be afraid of the strong Israelite tribes. Rather than use weapons and fight against them, he had a different idea: he would call upon a famous magician, named Balaam, to curse the Israelites. In those days, people believed that magic spells and curses could help defeat an enemy!

Balak sent a message to Balaam, calling him to his service. It said, "King Balak says to listen well. There are some people who have come from Egypt. They are so many, they cover the face of the earth. And even worse, they are camping near me! Come now, I beg you, and curse these people for me, for I know they are stronger than I am! If you do this, then perhaps I will be able to drive them out of the land. I know that you work magic and that whom you bless is blessed and whom you curse is cursed. Come and help me with this problem!"

The leading men of Moab, accompanied by neighbors from the country of Midian, set out to meet with Balaam and deliver the king's message. They carried all kinds of gifts, hoping to tempt the magician into helping the king with his problem:

There were lemon drops and licorice,
And jars full of gumdrops,
A sundial, a sunhat,
And sunflower seeds, too.
There were big, fluffy pillows,
And new silver sandals,
And beautiful candles,
Red, yellow, and blue.

When Balaam heard King Balak's request, he asked the men to stay overnight, saying, "Perhaps the Lord will come to me in a dream and help me with my answer."

197

During the darkest part of the night, God came to Balaam in a dream. "Who are these men with you?" He asked. Balaam told God about Balak's request.

God said to Balaam, "You may not go with them! You may not curse these people because they are blessed!"

In the morning, as he looked longingly at the gifts, Balak told the leaders, "Go back to your land; the Lord will not allow me to go with you."

When these unsuccessful men returned home, Balak the king sent an even more important group of leaders back to Balaam, to again try and convince him to come. They said, "King Balak says that he will give you great honors if you will help him. He will do anything that you ask, if only you will come and curse this people."

But Balaam answered, "Even if Balak gave me his own house full of silver and gold, I could not go against the word of the Lord. But stay here tonight; the Lord may speak to me in a dream, and you never know what He may say."

Balaam was keeping his options open; depending on what God said, he still might be able to collect the gifts and honors offered to him. During the darkest part of the night, God came to Balaam in a dream and said, "If these men have come to summon you, go with them. But you may say only the words that I tell you to say."

As the sun said hello to the world, Balaam saddled his donkey and followed the leaders of Moab and Midian. However, since God always knows what people are really thinking, He knew that Balaam was still hoping to get his hands on the rewards promised by King Balak. Because of this, God placed one of His angels on the road to bar Balaam's way.

When the donkey saw the angel of the Lord standing with his sword in hand, she turned aside and went into a field. Balaam, who saw nothing, smacked the donkey and tried to turn her back onto the road. Next, the angel of the Lord stood in a narrow path between the walls of two vineyards. When the donkey saw the angel of the Lord, she smashed Balaam's foot against the wall. Balaam, who saw nothing, howled with pain and again smacked

the donkey. The angel then went on ahead and stood in a place so narrow there was no room to turn left or right. When the donkey saw the angel of the Lord again, she lay down under Balaam and closed her eyes! Balaam, who saw nothing, smacked the donkey with his walking stick. That poor, old donkey!

But wonder of wonders! The Lord opened up the donkey's mouth and allowed her to speak to Balaam! She said, "What have I done to you that you have beaten me three times?"

A talking donkey is very unusual. Balaam the magician had never seen this trick before. Bewildered and confused, he replied to the donkey, "I smacked you because you made fun of me! I wish I had a sword in my hand now. I would kill you!"

The donkey laughed. It was funny to see her master so angry about seeing nothing! She said, "Aren't I your good old donkey that you have ridden upon all your life? Have I ever done anything like this to you before?"

Balaam, who was being almost as stubborn as a donkey, began to pout and answered with a loud "No!"

At that moment, the Lord opened the eyes of Balaam's mind, and Balaam saw the angel of the Lord standing in the way, sword in hand. Balaam gasped for breath, bowed his head, and fell flat on his face! The angel of the Lord said, "Why have you hit your poor, old donkey three times? It was I who stood in the road. Your donkey was smart enough to see me and she turned aside three times. If she hadn't turned aside, I would have killed you with my sword and let her live!"

Balaam said to the angel, "I have sinned! I saw nothing! I did not know that it was you who stood in my way!" All Balaam wanted was to go back home. He would be happy to give up his greedy thoughts! He had had enough! "If it displeases you," he told the angel, "I will go back."

"No," said the angel, "you must continue on with the men, and you may only say what I tell you to say." The angel of the Lord was sure that Balaam would now go as God's messenger and bless the Children of Israel.

The Messenger of God

Balaam went with the leaders to King Balak's country. "What took you so long?" asked the King. "I have promised you gifts and great honors."

Balaam said to King Balak, "I have come here to meet with you, but I can only say the words that God puts into my mouth."

The next morning, King Balak took Balaam to a high place where he could see some of the Children of Israel. Balaam told the king to prepare seven altars and fourteen burnt offerings and wait for him. He was hoping that if he went up to the nearest bare mountaintop, he would receive a message from God. As he stood alone in a high, windy spot, the Lord put these words in Balaam's mouth to say to King Balak:

"Balak, the King has brought me here
To curse the House of Jacob
And to predict a terrible doom
For a people whom God holds dear.
How can I curse those who God has not cursed?
How can I predict doom when God has not doomed?

From the top of these rocks
I see them living peacefully.
From the top of these hills
I see them living quietly.
They are people who always shall be set apart.
Who can count them?
Like dust they are,
All of them brothers.
May I die righteous, like these men,
With peace in my heart!"

When he heard the words that God had instructed Balaam to say, King Balak cried angrily, "What have you done to me? I brought you here to curse my enemies and you have blessed them instead!"

Balaam answered, "I must be careful to say only what the Lord has told me to say."

King Balak kept on trying; he desperately wanted Balaam's help and was used to getting his way. "Come with me to another place where you can see the other side of their camp. When you see these people, then you can curse them for me from there."

He took Balaam to a different mountaintop, built seven more altars, and offered up another fourteen burnt offerings. The king was working hard! Balaam said, "Wait here while I go and meet again with the Lord."

The Lord met Balaam in another high, windy spot and put these words in his mouth to say to King Balak:

> *"Hear me, King Balak,*
> *God is not man,*
> *Nor is He a son of man.*
> *He does not lie!*
> *He does not change his mind*
> *As the days go by!*
> *He does what He says He will*
> *When He has spoken;*
> *His words and His promises*
> *Never are broken!*
> *He has told me to bless them.*
> *I cannot reverse this;*
> *The Israelite people have done nothing wrong!*
> *The song of their trumpets*
> *Calls them to the Lord*
> *Who has brought them here safely,*
> *Far from Egypt's sword!"*

King Balak was furious. He threw a king's fit and shouted, "Neither curse them nor bless them!"

Balaam replied quietly, "Didn't I tell you that I must say only what the Lord has told me to say?"

King Balak scratched his crown and thought again. It took him a while till he came up with another idea, although it was not very original: Maybe a different place would change his luck. "Come now," he said, in a sweet voice that sounded like it was dripping with honey. "I will take you to a beautiful place. Perhaps it will please God to have you curse these people from there."

He took Balaam to the very top of Mount Peor; it gave a wonderful view of both the wilderness and the big Israelite camp. Balaam told King Balak to build seven more altars and prepare another fourteen burnt offerings. By this time, the king had taken off his crown and had tied a red bandanna around his sweating head!

This time, Balaam did not go away to be alone with God; he was beginning to know that God was pleased with him wherever he might be. As King Balak worked, grunting and groaning, he stayed where he was and looked out over the wide wilderness. He saw the Children of Israel in their orderly camp, tribe by tribe, flags flying in the desert breeze. The Spirit of God came over him and he said, in the words of one who has finally had his eyes opened all the way:

"How lovely are your tents, O Jacob,
Your dwellings, Israel, O how fair!
Your camps look like valleys,
Wide, green, and nice,
Like gardens by the waterside
Full of sweet spice.
And strong cedars beside
The clear waters reside.
Scattering seeds
With the wind and the tide.
Israel lies down,
It waits like a lion,
Peaceful yet watchful,
Protecting its might.
Blessed be those who bless you.
Cursed be those who curse you.
Let all who are enemies
Be prepared for a fight!"

King Balak's face was purple with rage! He started having a temper tantrum, stamping his feet and striking one fist against the other! "I called you to curse my enemies," he cried, "and here you have blessed them three times! Therefore, be quick! Leave! Go

home! I had planned to give you great honors and beautiful gifts, but the Lord has prevented you from receiving my rewards!"

And Balaam said to King Balak, "Didn't I tell your leaders that even if you offered me your house full of silver and gold, I could not go beyond the word of the Lord and do anything, good or bad, by myself? Whatever the Lord told me to say, I said. I will be glad to go back to my people, the quicker the better! But just this once, I will use my magician's powers and look into the future. I will tell you what these people, whom you have tried so hard to destroy, are going to do to you in days to come:

> "I see these people, the Children of Israel,
> And from their heart shall come a star,
> A mighty king,
> A ruler rising,
> Crushing their enemies near and far!"

King Balak went on his way, looking defeated and dusty. Balaam whistled for his now-silent, old donkey, climbed on her back, and with one more look at the wilderness full of hard-working, happy people, went home.

205

Deuteronomy

דברים

The Words of Moses

These are the words that Moses spoke to the Children of Israel,
As they waited for the Lord their God to take them by the hand,
Moses was their faithful leader,
Always working hard to help them be good people
And to find their way into the Promised Land.
Moses was an old man, though his eyes were not yet dim,
And he said, "Listen now, O Israel, to my words,
I shall begin:
Obey
The rules and regulations that I taught you long ago,
And when you go into Canaan
Those whom you meet will lift their eyes
And say
This great nation set before us is compassionate and wise.
What other nation has God close to it?
When we call Him, He is there,
But be careful and behave yourselves, be faithful and
Beware,
Lest you forget what you have seen:

The wonders and the signs, the day you stood before the Lord
On Mount Sinai, and you heard
The voice of God
Above the roar
Of thunder and of lightning,
And in that holy place He gave me tablets made of stone,
The Ten Commandments,
And He ordered me to make these lessons known:
'I am the Lord your God who brought you out of the land of Egypt.
You shall not have any other gods beside me.
You shall not make a sculpted image,
Of anything that is of heaven or of the earth or underwater.
You shall not swear falsely by God's name.
You must observe the Sabbath day and keep it holy
As the Lord has commanded you to do.
Remember that the Lord your God freed you
From Egypt with His hand
And His outstretched arm.
Therefore,
You must obey this strict command.
Honor your father and your mother
As the Lord your God commands you,
So that your family will live well
In this new land that God has given you.
You shall not murder.
You shall not commit adultery.
You shall not steal.
You shall not bear false witness.
You shall not covet your neighbor's wife,
Nor crave possessions not your own,
Your neighbor's field, his donkey, or his ox,
His money or his home.'

With a mighty voice God spoke these words
Aloud
Through cloud and darkness,
And upon two tablets made of stone
He wrote them down to make them known.
And then He told me to remain with Him and learn
These laws and rules.
So, if you want to go
Into the Promised Land,
Turn neither left nor right,
But walk the straight way of the Lord
And be holy in His sight."

Words of Faith

The Children of Israel listened carefully to Moses
As he gave them these directions,
Laws and rules and words of faith,
He said, "God gave me good instructions,
And these I give to you
So that you and your children
Live faithful lives
And obey them.
Then greatly may your families grow.
These laws and rules must not be broken
In the land where milk and honey flows,
The God of Israel has spoken!"

THE INSTRUCTIONS

Hear, O Israel!
The Lord your God,
The Lord is one.
And you shall love the Lord your God
With all your heart, your soul, and might,
And these words that I command you
Shall be written on your heart this day.
Teach them to your children,
Recite them in your homes,
Recite these words when you're away.
Recite them when you lie down,
Recite them when you rise.
Wrap these words around your hand,
Place them right between your eyes,
Put them on the doorposts of your house
And on the gates throughout your land.
And in days to come
When children ask the meaning of these laws,
Say, "It is because
In days gone by
We were slaves to Pharaoh,
And the Lord God, with His mighty hand,
And His outstretched arm,
Rescued us from Egypt
And brought us to the Promised Land."
The Lord commands us to observe His laws
And to remember them above
Whatever else we do in life.
This is the way we give God love.

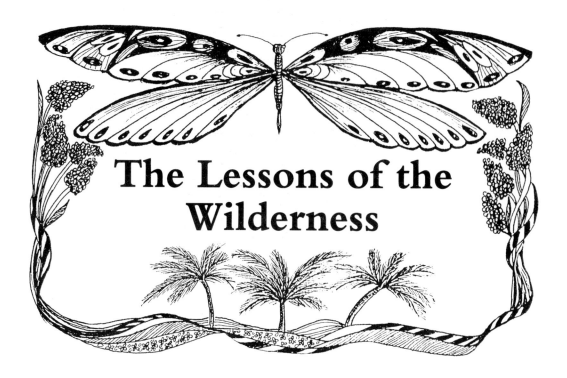

The Lessons of the Wilderness

Moses was a wonderful teacher; the Children of Israel were lucky to be his pupils! He patiently answered all their questions and he never made anyone feel bad. Sometimes he had to give lessons on very serious subjects, such as "How to Live the Good Life in the Promised Land." At these times, he stood on a high, flat rock and spoke to the entire camp. This way, he could see everyone, and everyone could see and hear him. Now that Aaron was gone, Moses had to do quite a bit of talking. When everyone was asleep, he stood on top of a hill and carefully practiced his speeches. Moses quickly taught himself to speak clearly and precisely. People can learn to do anything they want if they try hard enough.

Day after day, the Israelites waited to cross the Jordan River into their new land. And day after day, Moses continued to teach them God's lessons exactly as they had been given to him in the Tent of Meeting. Moses said to the Children of Israel:

"And you shall remember how you traveled forty years,
And how God tested you with hardships,
And how you bothered Him with tears.

214

The Lord tested you each day
To learn what lay inside your hearts,
And to see if you would follow his commands
Or turn away.
He made you hungry
And fed you sweet dew,
A food called 'Manna,' quite unknown,
To show that you can live as God decrees
And not by bread alone.

Your clothes did not wear out.
Your feet, though tired, did not swell.
As a father punishes a son
The Lord God punished you as well!
Therefore,
Keep the Commandments of the Lord,
Respect Him and walk in His ways,
For He is bringing you into a fine land,
A land of sunny days,
A good land filled with brooks and lakes and fountains,
Hills and valleys,
A land of wheat and barley, vines and figs,
And olive trees,
A land where food is plenty,
Wine and honey both abound,
A land whose stones are iron,
Where brass and copper can be found.
And when you have eaten and are full
You must thank God for all His goodness
And say
'We praise You God, King of the universe,
For food and loving-kindness.'
But if you forget the Lord, your God,
And fail to keep His Ten Commandments,
And fail to keep the other rules that I have
Taught you without cease,
When you've eaten and built houses,
When your herds and flocks increase,
When you have gold and you have silver,
Then beware you don't forget
The Lord, your God, who did deliver
You from Egypt,
With power terrible and strong,
And led you through the wilderness
To this fine land where you belong.
Do not say, 'My power

And my hand have won this wealth for me.'
Remember
It is God who gives you power
To be wealthy.
Do not forget the Lord your God.
There are no other gods to cherish.
You must listen only to His voice,
Or you shall surely perish!"

The Warnings

Moses taught the Israelites all kinds of lessons to memorize, names and numbers to remember, and many dos and don'ts. There were rules about eating and not eating certain foods, about observing holidays in God's honor, about how to behave properly in order to lead a good life and how to behave properly when someone dies.

Teaching the difference between right and wrong is a teacher's most important job. A good teacher is always honest with his or her pupils. Just because students are young does not mean they should be protected from knowing what might happen to them if rules and laws are disobeyed. But sometimes warnings sound like threats and threats sound like warnings. Both threats and warnings are useful only if the punishments they promise are carried out. Idle threats are foolish; after a while, nobody will believe a person who is constantly scaring others. However, whenever the Lord God gives a warning or makes a threat, the people who love and respect Him must absolutely take Him seriously. At the same time, when God promises His blessings, His people must do everything possible to live up to His expectations. These are some of the most important

218

lessons that Moses, the great teacher and friend of God, taught the Children of Israel.

And Moses said, "Now if you obey the Lord your God and faithfully observe all His commandments, rules, and laws that I will teach you today, then the Lord will set you high above all the nations of the earth. If you listen to the word of God, these blessings will come upon you like the sun, keeping you warm and helping you to lead a healthy life."

THE BLESSINGS AND THE CURSES

You shall be blessed in the city,
And you shall be blessed in the field.
Blessed shall be your children,
And may all your good land yield
Good harvests, and many offspring
From cattle and from sheep.
May your baskets, in which you carry
All the harvests that you reap,
Be blessed, and blessed too will be
The bowl that's used to knead the wheat.
Blessed shall be all your comings,
Blessed shall be your goings too,
Arrive safely, leave with kisses,
The Lord will take good care of you.
He will help defeat your enemies,
They'll flee before His mighty arm,
And He shall bless your work,
And bless your farms,
And keep them free from harm.
You shall be God's holy people,
He'll bless you, one and all, today
If you keep His commandments and His rules,
And walk only in His ways.
All the peoples of the earth shall see
God's name above you and respect you.

And they'll respect your work
And all the children
That the Lord will give you.
God will open up his heavens;
Your crops will never fail.
You shall owe no one,
They shall owe you,
The head you'll be
And not the tail.
These blessings shall be yours
If you turn neither left nor right.
But if you turn away and don't obey,
If you worship gods of stone,

Then the Lord shall bring these curses
Upon you and all you own:
You shall be cursed in the city,
You shall be cursed in the field.
Your basket and your kneading bowls
Shall be cursed and they shall yield
No produce from your land!
Your children shall be cursed,
Your animals as well,
Cursed be your comings and your goings
And the places where you dwell!
The Lord shall wipe out all your businesses
Because your evil ways
Caused you to forget Him
And He will bring you great dismay!
He will have plagues come down upon you,
Fevers, scorching heat, and droughts.
The skies will darken, they'll look like rust!
The sand will make the earth like dust!
Your enemies shall scatter you,
They'll rout you to far corners,
Birds and beasts shall eat you in a hurry,
There'll be no one left to bury!
Worms will eat your grapevines,
Olives will drop off the trees,
Locusts will destroy your seeds.
As for your children,
They will leave!
The stranger whom you helped
Shall be your master, without fail,
You will owe him,
He won't owe you,
He'll be the head, and you the tail!
All these curses shall befall you,
They will pursue and overtake,
Until you are wiped out!

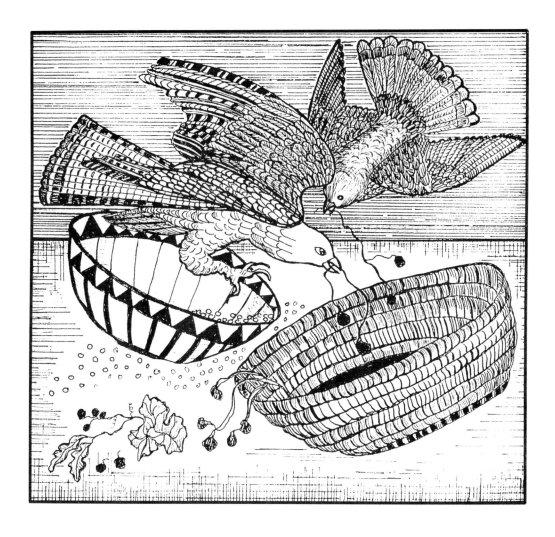

All these curses God will make
Come true,
Until you are no more,
Because you didn't listen to His voice
And obey His rules and laws!
And He will send you back to Egypt,
Where once your enemies did fall,
And no one there will want to buy you back!
This is the worst curse of them all!

A chill had come over the desert air. Nothing moved, not a blade of grass or a cow's ear. The Children of Israel were hardly breathing, so frightened were they by the list of curses that might

222

be brought upon them. In a quiet voice, Moses said, "See, I have given you lessons this day about life, wealth, death, and destruction. I order you, right now, to love the Lord your God, to walk in His ways, and keep His commandments, His laws, and His rules. This way you will live, have many children, and be blessed by the Lord your God as you enter the Promised Land. But if your heart turns away and you do not listen, and begin to worship gods of stone, then, I tell you truthfully, you will certainly perish! I call heaven and earth to be witnesses today and hear these words: I have put before you life and death, blessings and curses. Choose life—if you and your children want to live—by loving the Lord your God, obeying His commands, and being faithful to Him! This way you shall have a good, long life in the land that the Lord your God promised Abraham, Isaac, and Jacob to give to you!"

The Song of Moses

God's blessings and curses had been an exhausting lesson to teach, and Moses felt the need for some cool, fresh air. He left the Children of Israel alone with their thoughts and took a walk in the hills. Everyone needs some quiet time for thinking and calming down. The Children of Israel needed some quiet time to understand all that they had learned. They also needed some time to prepare themselves to behave properly in the Promised Land.

When the camp returned to its normal, noisy activities, Moses once again called all the tribes together. What he had to say now was extremely important! "I am one hundred and twenty years old," said Moses, slowly and carefully. "My bones are tired and I can no longer be active." The whole camp was alarmed! They never thought of Moses as old.

He continued, "The Lord has told me that I shall not cross over the Jordan river into the Promised Land. The Lord, Himself, will cross over before you and will destroy your enemies. The Lord has commanded Joshua to be your new leader!"

Then Moses called Joshua to come up and stand with him. He

told Joshua, right in front of the Children of Israel, "Be strong and have courage because it is you who will go with these people into the land that the Lord promised their ancestors He would give them. You shall divide it up fairly for them. The Lord will be with you. He will not fail you. Do not fear and do not worry!" Joshua stood tall, his shoulders back and his head held high.

Then Moses wrote down everything that God had taught him, all the Teachings, the rules and the laws. He gave this scroll of writing to the Levite priests, who carried the Ark of the Covenant. He also made sure that the Israelite leaders would be able to see and read the holy words. This way, these Teachings would be available to all the people for study and learning.

The Lord said to Moses, "The time is drawing near for you to die. Call Joshua and bring him to the Tent of Meeting so that I may give him instructions." Moses and Joshua presented themselves, as God requested. The Lord appeared in a pillar of cloud and said to Moses, "You are soon to go and lie with your ancestors. I am still afraid that this people will go astray and not remember all that I have told you to teach them. Therefore, write down this poem and teach it to the Children of Israel. Make them learn it by heart!"

And the Lord said to Joshua, "Be strong and have courage, for you shall bring the Israelites into the Promised Land!" Joshua was overwhelmed! He felt both happy and unhappy. On the one hand, he was honored to be chosen by God to be the new leader; on the other hand, he was saddened and sorry to know that Moses would soon be leaving forever. But no matter how he felt inside, Joshua promised himself that he would work hard and do his very best to make sure that the Children of Israel arrived safely in their new home.

That same day, Moses wrote down God's poem so that he might teach it to the Israelites. When he had also put in writing each and every one of the other Teachings, he said to the Levites, "Take this book and place it beside the Ark of the Covenant of the Lord your God. This shall be its resting place."

Then Moses recited all the words of God's poem. The whole congregation of Israel listened and remembered it:

Give ear, O heavens, and let me speak,
Let the earth hear the words I say,
May my words pour like rain,
Like droplets on grass.
Give glory to God.
The Lord's name I proclaim!.

His deeds are perfect, His ways are just,
He is a faithful God, upright and true.
Remember the old days,
Consider the past,
He gave the nations their homes
And showed them His ways!

226

He found the Israelites in a desert.
And He carried them like children.
Like an eagle, He was their guide.
And He swooped down!
They lay beneath His wings.
No false god at His side!

He set His people on high ground.
They ate the food from all around.
They feasted and ate honey,
There was olive oil and milk,
Lambs and rams and fine ground wheat,
And grape wine smooth as silk.

But the Israelites grew fat,
They were loaded down by food,
And they forgot the God who made them,
Who helped their children grow.
They made gods of gold,
And angered Him,
Who rescued them from Pharaoh.

The Lord saw and He was angered!
He ignored His sons and daughters.
He said, "I will hide My Glory from them,
And see how they fare in the end.
They have no loyalty in them!

"The wine for them will be from Sodom,
From the vineyards of Gomorrah!
Their grapes will be poisoned,
Their wine like a snake bite!
I have put these things away
Because
I might use them some day!"

The Lord will have His revenge,
When He sees their might is gone.
He will say, "Where are their gods of stone
Who they turned to, seeking help?
Let them shield you when you're all alone!
You'll see that I am He!
There is no other god beside Me!

"I deal death and I give life.
I wound and I will heal.
I raise my hand to heaven on high
And say,
'As I live forever,
When My hand gives out judgment,
I shall revenge My foes!
Those people who reject Me:
They will surely die!' "

Sing aloud, O you nations of Israelites,
He will punish you
If you disobey!
And He will punish His enemies,
And clear out the guilty,
From the land that He gives to His people today!

When Moses finished reciting all these words to the Children of Israel, he said, "Take to heart all these words of warning! Teach them to your children, so they may faithfully follow all of this teaching. For this is not a small, empty thing for you: it is your very life! And through it you will live good, long lives in the land that you are about to enter."

That very same day, the Lord said to Moses, "Climb Mount Nebo, in the land of Moab facing Jericho. I want you to see the land of Canaan that I am giving to the Children of Israel as their possession. You shall die on the mountain that you are about to climb, as your brother Aaron did on Mount Hor. This is because

228

you both broke faith with Me in the wilderness and doubted My word. You may see the land from a distance, but you shall not enter it!"

The Lord God had followed through on His threats and warnings. Moses, the friend of God, understood and accepted his punishment. He lifted his eyes and looked over the whole camp. Flags were flying, people were washing clothes and cooking, cows and goats were being milked, and children were everywhere, getting into everything, and bothering nobody. With prayers for their future happiness tucked inside his wise, old heart, Moses began to say his good-byes.

Farewell to Moses

Standing on a high, flat rock, Moses, the great teacher and man of God, said his last words to the Children of Israel. He gave separate blessings to all the different tribes. Everyone, grown-ups and children, birds, animals, and even lizards bowed their heads in respect to Moses, their wise teacher and good friend. Then, filled with love for his people, Moses gave them his very last blessing:

"O Children of Israel,
There is none like the Lord
Who rides through the heavens to help you.
God is your refuge,
A place for you to dwell,
His arms will support you
And your children as well.
He drove out your enemies,
His command was, 'Destroy!'
And this people called Israel,
Every girl, every boy,

Will be safe in His hand
In their sunny new land
Full of fine grain and wine,
Figs, olives, and honey,
Under heavens that drop dew!
Happy people,
Who is like you?
A people saved by the Lord,
Your shield,
And your sword!''

As the sun wrapped its warm smile around the earth, the old moon rose and hung like a locket in the pale, blue sky. Lambs snuggled close to their mothers. Chickens and ducks covered their little ones with wide, feathery wings. Donkeys stopped pushing each other, and the camels started to behave like ladies and gentlemen. Thousands and thousands of people quietly lined the path that Moses took as he went up to the mountain, as the Lord had commanded. The eyes that followed him were bright with tears of joy and tears of sadness: the joy of having known such a wonderful man as Moses, and the sadness of saying good-bye to him.

As Moses began his walk, his great-great-grandchildren ran up to him crying, "Grandfather Moses! Wait! We have gifts for you!"

Moses said, "You are all my gifts. I need nothing else!"

"But Grandfather," they replied, "they are gifts to take along with you and keep forever!"

Then two dark-haired little girls came forward, carrying a large, white, wool shawl, threaded with silver and gold. In each of the four corners was a fringe of blue thread.

"The weavers made this for you, Grandfather," they said proudly, handing it to him.

"What a beautiful shawl!" exclaimed Moses, wrapping himself in its great warmth. "Every time I wear it and see its fringes, I shall remember God's commandments. Thank you very much!"

231

Next, a little boy shyly came up to Moses. He was carrying a bag embroidered with flowers and butterflies.

He said softly, "In this bag are two leather boxes with long straps attached, made by my father. Inside them you will find the words of the Lord. One box you place on your arm, close to your heart, to remind you of God's outstretched arm; the other you can place between your eyes, close to your mind."

"How wonderful!" said Moses. "Thank you very much!"

Another little boy ran up to Moses, hugged him, and wouldn't let go. "Don't forget to give Grandfather your gift," whispered his mother.

"Oh, I'm sorry," said the child. "Here, Grandfather, is a beautiful gift from our best silversmith."

Moses unwrapped the present and saw an intricately carved silver case. A parchment, with God's words on it, written by a scribe, was rolled up inside. When he looked closely, Moses could see the word "Almighty" written on the back.

"You must place it on the right doorpost of your new home," said the little boy.

"I most certainly intend to!" answered Moses. "Thank you very much!"

With a big smile, Moses waved a last good-bye. "You have made this a happy day for me!" he said to all the Children of Israel. "Be strong, my people, and strengthen yourselves!"

Wrapped in his white shawl with blue fringes, and carrying his new embroidered bag that held the two leather boxes full of God's words and the shiny silver case for the doorpost of heaven, Moses went up to Mount Nebo. Though he was old, his eyes were not dim.

The Lord showed him the Promised Land, the mountains, the valleys, the rivers, and the cities of palm trees. And the Lord said to Moses, "This is the land that I promised Abraham, Isaac, and Jacob I would give to their descendants. You have now seen it with your own eyes!"

Moses stood on the mountaintop and looked at the land for just another moment. And then, as the sun hid its face and the tiny, sweet tears of angels wet his cheeks, Moses disappeared. The great, gray cloud had come down and closed around him like sheltering arms, and Moses was taken away with a kiss.

And never again did there arise in Israel a man like Moses, whom the Lord knew face to face!

About the Author

Esta Cassway is a painter, printmaker, and writer. She studied at the Philadelphia College of Art and received a Bachelor of Fine Arts from the Tyler School of Fine Art, Temple University. Esta Cassway's work has appeared in *The Jewish Exponent, Inside Magazine,* and *The Temple Review,* Temple University. She is also known for her performances of her own narratives, nostalgic essays and poems, as well as numerous one-person exhibits of her art. The mother of three grown sons, Esta Cassway lives in Wyncote, Pennsylvania, a suburb of Philadelphia, with her husband Robert, an architect. She is currently at work on a companion volume to *The Five Books of Moses for Young People* dealing with Prophets and Writings.